LAND AND PEASANTS IN CENTRAL LUZON

Land and Peasants in Central Luzon

SOCIO-ECONOMIC STRUCTURE OF A PHILIPPINE VILLAGE

BY AKIRA TAKAHASHI

EAST-WEST CENTER PRESS   HONOLULU
in cooperation with the Institute of Developing Economies, Tokyo

Copyright © in Japan, 1969
by the Institute of Developing Economies
42, Honmura-cho, Ichigaya, Shinjuku-ku, Tokyo

First published in Japan, 1969
by the Institute of Developing Economies

Published outside Japan, 1970
East-West Center Press, Honolulu
Standard Book Number: 8248-0088-5
Printed and bound in Japan

PREFACE

The present monograph, based on a field survey of a rice-growing village in the Central Luzon Plain conducted by the writer during a 10-month period from 1963 to 1964, is aimed at an analysis of the basic type of socio-economic structure in the rural Philippines. In the survey the writer tried to observe every aspect of productive activity and life in the village as minutely as possible. He sought, especially, to understand the actual situation of the land system, agricultural production, and the labor force. Thus, an approach has been made to understand the problems confronting Philippine agriculture and rural society.

The Japanese edition of this monograph, *Chūbu Luzon no beisaku nōson* (A Rice-Growing Village in Central Luzon), was published by the Institute of Asian Economic Affairs as its Research Paper No. 85 in July 1965. The present monograph is an English translation of the revised Japanese original.

The writer's interest in village structure in the Central Luzon Plain and his desire for a long-term participant survey were engendered while he was studying the subject of "Agricultural Development in the Philippine Islands" on a scholarship of the Philippine Board of Scholarship for Southeast Asia, University of the Philippines, from 1958 to 1960. During his first stay, the writer obtained some insight into the fundamental problems in Philippine agriculture and their regional characteristics through extensive observations throughout the Philippine Islands. During his second visit he settled in a small village in the major agricultural area for an extended period and conducted intensive observation of the community.

The present monograph was made possible by the generous assistance, advice, suggestion and encouragement of a great many people. The writer is particularly indebted to Dr. Enrique Virata, Professor Emeritus, University of the Philippines and the former Chairman, Community Development Research Council of the same university, for making research facilities available to him, and to the members and staff of the Council for their valuable suggestions. The writer's heartfelt acknowledgment is due to all the villagers of Barrio Kabukiran for their understanding of, and cooperation with, his work. He also would like to thank townspeople and officials of the Municipality of Baliuag, especially his neighbors of Barrio Virgen de las Flores, for their hospitality to him and his wife.

Atty. Rogaciano Mercado, Member of the Congress, Republic of the Philippines; Dr. Milton Barnett, Agricultural Development Council; Dr. Ruben Santos-Cuyugan, Director, Institute of Asian Studies, University of the Philippines and the present Chairman, Community Development Research Council; Mr. Jose Domingo, Asian Labor Education Center, University of the Philippines; Mr. Pacifico Bautista, Provincial Agriculturalist, Bulacan; and Mr. Alfredo Dimaano, Agricultural Productivity Commission, all offered a great amount of valuable advice and help which is deeply appreciated by the writer. He is also thankful to Mr. Cesar Deciderio and his family, and Mrs. Adela Lapeña and her family of Baliuag, Bulacan, for their many kindnesses; he and his wife owe them comfortable and memorable days in the municipality.

The writer would like to express his gratitude to Dr. TŌBATA Seiichi, President, the Institute of Asian Economic Affairs, both for offering him the opportunity for fieldwork in the Philippines and for encouraging him to publish this English edition of the monograph. His thanks also go to his colleagues in the Institute of Asian Economic Affairs, especially to Mr. TAKIGAWA Tsutomu and other members of the Philippine study group, for their valuable comments on the monograph. He owes a special debt of gratitude to Dr. IIZUKA Koji, Professor Emeritus, University of Tokyo, and Prof. ŌNO Morio, the Institute of Oriental Culture, University of Tokyo, for their advice on problems concerning methodology.

Further, the writer wishes to express his profound thanks to Mr. HOSHINO Ikumi for his competent assistance in translating the text into English. He is also deeply grateful to Prof. James E. Landes of Aoyama Gakuin University for reading the manuscript and suggesting changes in expression. Finally he would like to record the debt he owes to his wife Mitsuko for her patience and constant help at the time of field investigations as well as for her devoting many hours to typing and other tasks at all stages of preparation of this monograph.

Tokyo   TAKAHASHI Akira
April 1968

Contents

PART I. INTRODUCTION

PART II. BARRIO KABUKIRAN, 1963-64

viii

PART III. LAND AND PEASANTS IN CENTRAL LUZON: GENERALIZED CONCLUSIONS

List of Tables, Figures and Maps

TABLE

GENERAL NOTES

1. The name of the Barrio surveyed and those of villagers in the Barrio are fictitious.

2. Part II of this monograph describes the findings of the survey conducted in Barrio Kabukiran from 1963 to 1964. Consequently the use of present tense in Part II indicates the situation which was prevailing at that time.

3. In this series the surname of Japanese is given in capital letters and comes first, except in references to published works in English where the author's name is given in the reverse order.

4. Since 1961 one peso (=100 centavos) has been equivalent to about 0.256 U.S. dollar.

PART I
INTRODUCTION

CHAPTER I

Problems and Procedure of the Survey

The study of Philippine agriculture has been pushed since World War II. This has been partly because of the need to cope with the growing social unrest in the postwar period rooted primarily in rural problems, and partly because an increase in agricultural productivity has been regarded as a prerequisite to economic development. Industrialization in the Philippines which had showed marked progress after Independence has been slowed by the bottleneck of too small a domestic market. Furthermore, the unfavorable international balance of payments resulting from changes in foreign trade structure has been aggravated by the continued need for food imports till quite recently. Under such circumstances, to increase domestic agricultural production, which has tended to be stagnant, has come to be considered a key to economic development.

To understand the rural problems, a study of three factors is required: landownership and stratifying differentials in the landed class; disintegration of the peasantry and the class structure in rural villages; and the direction of peasants' movements.[1] It is important to analyze the actual situations of surplus population in villages and of the structure of rural society. Hence, the accumulation of studies concerning the socio-economic structure of villages, based on intensive field surveys, is needed.

Several introductory studies of Philippine villages were published before World War II, including the classic work on rural society by Le Roy.[2] Studies based on field surveys at the level of rural villages, however, were focused on the ethnology of tribal communities. It was only after World

---

[1]TAKAHASHI Akira, "Firippin nōgyō no dōkō (Recent Changes of the Philippine Agriculture)," *Tōyō bunka*, No. 30 (1961), 102-103.

[2]James A. Le Roy, *Philippine Life in Town and Country* (New York, 1905).

War II that analyses of economic and social structure in lowland villages began to be published for the first time. The pioneering work was field surveys conducted by a group of social scientists under the auspices of the United States Mutual Security Agency. Initiated because of the political problem of growing rural unrest, these studies aimed at constructing the whole image of rural society. Uniform surveys were conducted of sample villages selected from throughout the country,[3] and especially in Central Luzon,[4] which was considered to be the focus of the rural problems. However, the analysis of the relationship between social relations and production relations in particular villages remains to be completed.

While ethnographic researches on tribesmen in Mountain Province, Mindanao, Mindoro and other areas have been continued, in recent years the study of acculturation in rural settlements by cultural anthropologists has been making rapid strides. Many communities selected for study are still those in mountainous areas, but the number of studies dealing with lowland rural society has been increasing.[5] Among these are the analyses of social structure in relation to economic stratification and political power in Philippine villages.[6]

Compared with such achievements in the fields of anthropology and sociology, the contribution of agricultural economics to the study of socioeconomic structure in villages is still meager. The number of case studies on farm management at the level of rural settlements has been increasing,[7]

[3]Generoso Rivera and Robert McMillan, *The Rural Philippines* (Manila, 1952).

[4]Rivera and McMillan, *An Economic and Social Survey of Rural Households in Central Luzon* (Manila, 1954).

[5]For example, Donn V. Hart, "Barrio Caticugan: A Visayan Filipino Community," (dissertation, Syracuse Univ., 1954); Richard W. Coller, *Barrio Gacao, a Study of Village Ecology and the Schistosomiasis Problems* (Quezon City, 1960); Ethel Nurge, *Life in a Leyte Village* (Seattle, 1965); W. F. Nydegger and C. Nydegger, *Tarong: An Ilocos Barrio in the Philippines* (New York, 1966); W. E. Sibley, "Economy, Social Organization and Directed Cultural Change: The Philippines." Paper read at the Symposium on Modernization of Rural Areas, Eleventh Pacific Science Congress, Tokyo, August 1966.

[6]James N. Anderson analyzes social stratification in a village in the central part of the Province of Pangasinan, "Land and Society in a Pangasinan Community," *Philippine Soicological Review*, X-1, 2 (1962), 41-58. In her *The Dynamics of Power in a Philippine Municipality* (Quezon City, 1965), Mary R. Hollnsteiner makes an incisive analysis of the political power structure in the Province of Bulacan.

[7]For example, V. U. Quintana, "Palay Marketing Practices of Farmers in Gapan and San Antonio, Nueva Ecija, 1955-1956," *Philippine Agriculturist*, XLI (1957), 327-343; G. R. Vega, "The Expenditures of Incomes of 100 Families in Canlalay, Biñan, Laguna, 1955," *Philippine Agriculturist*, XLI (1957), 344-356; T. B. Balinguit, "Palay Marketing on the Farm Level in Nueva Ecija, 1955-1956," *Philippine Agriculturist*, XLII (1958), 18-35; C. U. Caintic et al., *Management Practices, Costs and Returns of Sugar Cane Farms in the Victorias Milling District* (College, Laguna, 1962).

but only a few have gone so far as to analyze the relationship between economic problems and structure of rural society. The detailed survey report on three sample farming households in the Province of Laguna, one such recent study, deserves special attention in that it provides interesting data on farm economy and village life.[8] In this connection also, the Community Development Research Council, University of the Philippines, should be highly commended for its role in the development of studies of Philippine villages. The Council has been publishing a large number of excellent monographs on the problems relating to the development of agricultural production and to modernization of rural communities, based on intensive field surveys.[9]

Although a considerable number of monographs on rural communities have been published in recent years, only a few have attempted to relate social relations adequately to production relations from the perspective of socio-economic history, and few give adequate answers to the problems of village structure as mentioned before. The further accumulation of detailed observations, therefore, is needed for an understanding of the socio-economic structure of villages in the Philippines.

It is for the reasons mentioned above that the writer conducted a field survey. However, at this point, he would like to touch briefly on some of the major problems in rural structure as he came across them in the analysis of data preparatory to the field survey.[10]

It is well known that in the Philippines a large number of peasants had been deprived of land in the early twentieth century because of development of agricultural production for the market, which began in the early nineteenth century. In the 1920's, when cash crop agriculture developed full-fledged as the supplier of raw materials for the United States, the concentration of landholding was accelerated. Since then the increase of non-farming population without landholdings in villages, as well as of tenant farmers, has been marked.[11] It is true that in Philippine villages

---

[8]Ralph C. Diaz et al., Case Studies of Farm Families, Laguna Province, Philippines (College, Laguna, 1960).

[9]For example, Coller, Barrio Gacao; P. Covar, The Masagana/Malgate System of Planting Rice: A Study of an Agricultural Innovation (1960); Hollnsteiner, Dynamics; T. V. Tiglao, Health Practices in a Rural Community (1964).

[10]TAKAHASHI, "Firippin nōson shakai no jakkan no mondai (Problems Relating to the Peasantry Disintegration in the Philippine Rural Society)," Kaigai jijō, XI-8 (1963), 38-45.

[11]According to a survey by Rivera and McMillan in 1952, laborers accounted for 47 per cent of the labor force in rural areas whereas farm holders (owner farmers and tenants) accounted for 22 per cent (Rural Philippines, p.168).

not only large estates but also small-size farming households need hired labor; but it seems that the required labor is only a small fraction of the large surplus of labor in the villages.

Then, what forms of existence does the wage labor force in villages assume? To answer this question, analysis of social relations in the villages, especially the structure of village communities and of families, is required. Rural society in the Philippines today is undoubtedly based on rural settlements, barrios, as the basic units; to what extent does the barrio retain communal relationships as basic organizing principles? Irrigation has been one of the factors in communal unity in other countries in Monsoon Asia; what kind of role does irrigation play in the Philippine villages? Labor exchange among farming households is often cited as an example of the communal character of the Philippine villages; is such labor exchange an important factor in farm production? Economic interdependence remains as the strong tie binding Filipino families and kins; what kind of function does it play in the problems of surplus population? The answers to these questions must be found in the relationship between social relations and economic structure.

The purpose of the survey, on which the present monograph was based, was to grasp the actualities of interrelations between economic structure and social relations by means of firsthand observation of a particular village and thereby to approach an understanding of the problems mentioned above. The writer concentrated his research on a small village because he wanted to understand problems confronting Philippine villages from the inside rather than from outside, by as close observation as possible, and at the same time to obtain intimate knowledge about every aspect of production and life in Philippine villages. This kind of understanding would be, of course, the common knowledge of Filipino students of rural society, but would be emphasized consciously by a foreign observer. In the survey, therefore, considerable importance was attached to experiential elements such as living in the village and establishing rapport with villagers through long-term contacts with them.

The area surveyed was selected from the rice-growing region in the Central Luzon Plain. Rice-growing is the most important farm production in the Philippines, and Central Luzon is the largest agricultural zone of the country. Furthermore, this region has been for long the focus of rural problems. The Municipality of Baliuag, Province of Bulacan, was finally decided on as the site of the survey because (1) it is located in the Tagalog-speaking region, so that this writer's knowledge of Tagalog could be utilized; (2) it is covered by a large irrigation system and is supposed to belong to the advanced agricultural zone; (3) its location on the fringe of Manila's commuter zone makes it easy to observe the outflow of the labor force from villages; but (4) it is not so near to Manila as to be greatly influenced by urbanization.

A discription of the survey procedure follows. In November 1963 a preliminary survey of the Municipality of Baliuag was begun, and in December this writer and his wife rented and settled in a small nipa house in Barrio Virgen de las Flores on the west edge of the town-proper of the Municipality of Baliuag. In January 1964 this writer decided on Barrio Kabukiran as the site of his intensive survey, and he was introduced to villagers of Barrio Kabukiran by a primary school teacher who had once served in the barrio school in the village. He commuted two kilometers to the Barrio by bicycle. During the first few months, he made special efforts to establish rapport with the villagers utilizing his knowledge of local language and at the same time observed farm work. Meanwhile, he collected basic data regarding the village and villagers by himself. Since an accurate map of the village, let alone an aerial photo, was not available, the writer made a map of the village to a scale of 1:5,000 by means of a Brunton compass and a pedometer, and made great efforts to obtain positive data on topographical conditions, land use, the size of farms, and landholding.

Taking pictures of villagers and distributing copies to them helped to identify the family composition and the existence of migratory workers, as well as to foster friendship with the villagers. Only after intimate rapport with the villagers was established, did this writer begin his investigation into the economy of individual household. For about three months at this stage of the survey the writer hired an interpreter to ask rather delicate questions to villagers. The interpreter was a college graduate who lived in Barrio Virgen de las Flores and was on the waiting list for the job of school teacher. This writer was keenly aware of various defects which have been caused by employing an interpreter and, therefore, made efforts to rectify such defects by other means. In interviewing the villagers, he did not use questionnaires,[12] but tried instead through free conversations to understand what kinds of problems they were faced with and what they thought about such problems. The survey was completed

---

[12]This writer appreciates usefulness of the questionnaires. However, he is rather inclined to attach great importance to personal dialogue with each villager and to flexibility of range of the investigation.

at the end of August 1964.[13] In addition, a three-day auxiliary survey was conducted in December 1965.

The survey covered economic and social relations in the village and special attention was focused on the following items: (1) farm production, and conditions curtailing increase in productivity; (2) landownership and landlord-tenant relations; (3) employment structure, especially of wage workers and farm holders; (4) communal relations; (5) relations concerning water use; and (6) family and kinship relations.

[13]Between September 1964 and November 1965 the writer was engaged in field-works in India. The observations of Indian rural areas were really helpful to bring about a better understanding of the Philippine villages.

CHAPTER II

An Outline of the Area Surveyed

The Central Luzon Plain

The Central Luzon Plain is a vast plain surrounded by the two mountain ranges, Sierra Madre and Zambales, and the two bays, Manila Bay and Lingayen Gulf; it stretches over the five provinces of Bulacan, Pampanga, Tarlac, Nueva Ecija, and Pangasinan. It is the largest agricultural zone in the Philippines and contains 567 thousand hectares of arable land or 10.3 per cent of the country's total.

Table 1 and Table 2 show the land use and agricultural situations in the Central Luzon Plain, as of 1960, indicating the extremely high proportion of rice-growing in farm production. The average ratio of the areas planted to palay (unhulled rice or rice plant) including double-cropping to the total arable land in the five provinces of Central Luzon was 93.5 per cent, about twice the national average; this ratio was highest (105 per cent) in Bulacan and lowest (88 per cent) in Pangasinan; all this indicates that palay was the crop of primary importance. Next to palay in importance was corn; the ratio of the area planted to corn to the total

Table 1. Principal Crops in Central Luzon (1960)

	Total net area planted in 1,000 ha.	Area planted in 1,000 ha.				Production of palay in 1,000 cavans*
		Palay*	Corn	Sugar-cane	Coconut	
Philippines	5,580.2	2,730.4	1,902.0	176.3	1,497.0	73,990.6
Total of 5 provinces	567.7	530.6	40.9	31.4	8.0	18,180.0
Bulacan	64.5	67.7	1.9	0.5	0	2,308.0
Pampanga	80.6	73.6	1.8	15.7	0	2,590.1
Tarlac	105.9	97.1	3.6	13.1	0.5	3,275.0
Neuva Ecija	175.3	167.3	12.6	0.1	0.3	6,442.0
Pangasinan	141.4	124.9	20.9	2.0	7.1	3,564.4

* See Appendix B.
Source: Census of the Philippines, 1960

Table 2. Agriculture in Central Luzon (1960)

	Percentage of area planted to palay to total net area planted	Percentage of irrigated land to total farm area	Percentage of farms using chemical fertilizer to total farms	Yield of palay per hectare (cavans)	Average size of farms (ha.)	Tenure of farms in percentage			
						Full owners	Part-owners	Tenants	Managers & others
Philippines	48.9	8.0	13.7	27.1	3.6	44.7	14.4	39.9	1.0
Average of 5 provinces	93.5	31.1	36.9	32.0	2.8	19.5	14.4	64.8	1.3
Bulacan	105.0	27.6	38.6	34.1	2.3	18.0	11.9	69.1	1.0
Pampanga	91.3	39.9	39.3	35.2	3.2	8.0	4.4	85.2	2.4
Tarlac	91.7	28.7	45.7	33.7	3.2	18.8	15.2	62.2	3.7
Nueva Ecija	95.4	33.4	50.6	38.5	3.7	14.5	8.0	76.3	1.2
Pangasinan	88.4	26.8	22.8	28.5	1.9	27.2	22.3	50.1	0.3

Source: Census of the Philippines, 1960

arable land was 14.9 per cent in Pangasinan and 6.9 per cent in Nueva Ecija. Third in importance was sugarcane; the ratio of the area planted to sugarcane to the total arable land was 19.4 per cent in Pampanga and 12.4 per cent in Tarlac.

Thus, in the Central Luzon Plain rice was, and still is, the most important crop and rice-growing is the basic farming pattern. Rice-growing in Central Luzon is also of national importance in that the five provinces accounted for 19.4 per cent of the country's planted area of palay and for 24.6 per cent of the national rice production in 1960. The Central Luzon Plain really deserves to be called the "rice granary of the Philippine Islands."

Agriculture in the Central Luzon Plain was in a relatively advanced stage in 1960. The ratio of irrigated land to the total arable land was high, about four times the national average. The use of fertilizers was widespread, and the proportion of farming households which applied chemical fertilizers, however small in amount, to their farms was nearly three times the national average. Yield of palay per hectare in each of the five provinces was higher than the national average.

The salient fact in production relations was the prevalence of the tenant system. The average size of farms was small, and the proportion

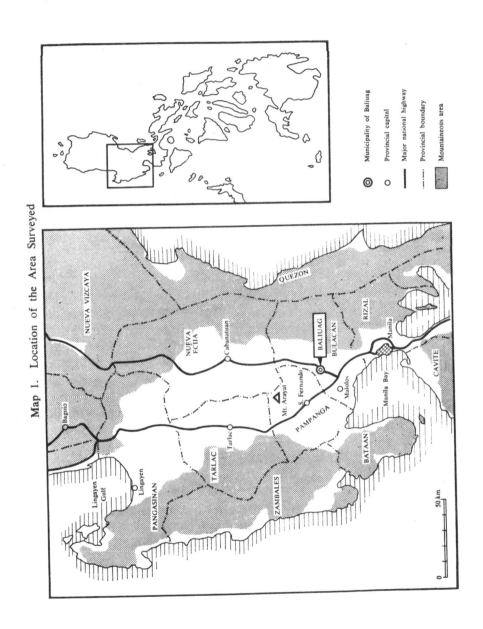

Map 1. Location of the Area Surveyed

Municipality of Baliuag
Provincial capital
Major national highway
Provincial boundary
Mountaineous area

QUEZON
NUEVA VIZCAYA
NUEVA ECIJA
Cabanatuan
RIZAL
BALIUAG
BULACAN
Manila
S. Fernando
Mt. Arayat
CAVITE
PAMPANGA
Malolos
Manila Bay
Baguio
Tarlac
BATAAN
TARLAC
ZAMBALES
Lingayen Gulf
Lingayen
PANGASINAN

0   50 km

of tenant farms was extremely high. While the average national ratio of tenant farms to all farms was about 40 per cent, the corresponding average ratio in the five provinces was 65 per cent, with the ratio in the Province of Pampanga being 85 per cent. If the number of part-owner farms was added to the number of tenant farms, the average ratio of such farms to the total farms in the five provinces was more than 81 per cent.

The Central Luzon Plain has been the focus of rural problems in the Philippines. In the late nineteenth century it played an important role in the Philippine Revolution, and since then agrarian unrest has repeatedly occurred in the region. Especially in the 1940's and early 1950's when flames of the Hukbalahap-HMB[1] uprisings flared up, the Provinces of Pampanga, Bulacan, and Nueva Ecija were the very center of the movement. Mt. Arayat rising in the midst of the plain and the Candaba Swamp at its foot served as symbolic hideouts for the Huks.

The Municipality of Baliuag

The Municipality of Baliuag in the Province of Bulacan is located in the southern part of the Central Luzon Plain, 50 kilometers northeast of Manila (Map 1). Since it is served by the national highway linking Manila with Cagayan Valley, transportation is relatively convenient. One can go from Baliuag to Manila in an hour and a half by bus. The frequency of bus service between Baliuag and Manila is several times an hour. The municipality is also traversed by a branch line of the Manila Railroad leading to Peñaranda, Nueva Ecija, and three trains are run every day. Those who live in the town-proper can commute to Manila, and there are many people who work in Manila on weekdays and return to their homes in Baliuag on weekends.

The population of the Municipality of Baliuag was 37,409 at the 1960 census, an increase of 22 per cent over 1948. The rate of population increase in Baliuag was considerably lower than the provincial average (35 per cent) and the national average (44 per cent) in the corresponding period. The inhabitants are Tagalogs; the number of Chinese in 1960 was only 80. The number of barrio[2] had been 18 until 1960; afterwards

---

[1] In 1948 the Hukbalahap was reorganized and renamed *Hukbong Mapagpalaya ng Bayan* (HMB), or the National Army of Liberation.

[2] The province is divided into municipalities, and each municipality comprises many barrios. In 1960 the Province of Bulacan consisted of 24 municipalities, and the total number of barrios in the province was 443 (the number of barrios in each municipality ranged from seven to 46).

Map 2. Municipality of Baliuag and Its Barrios

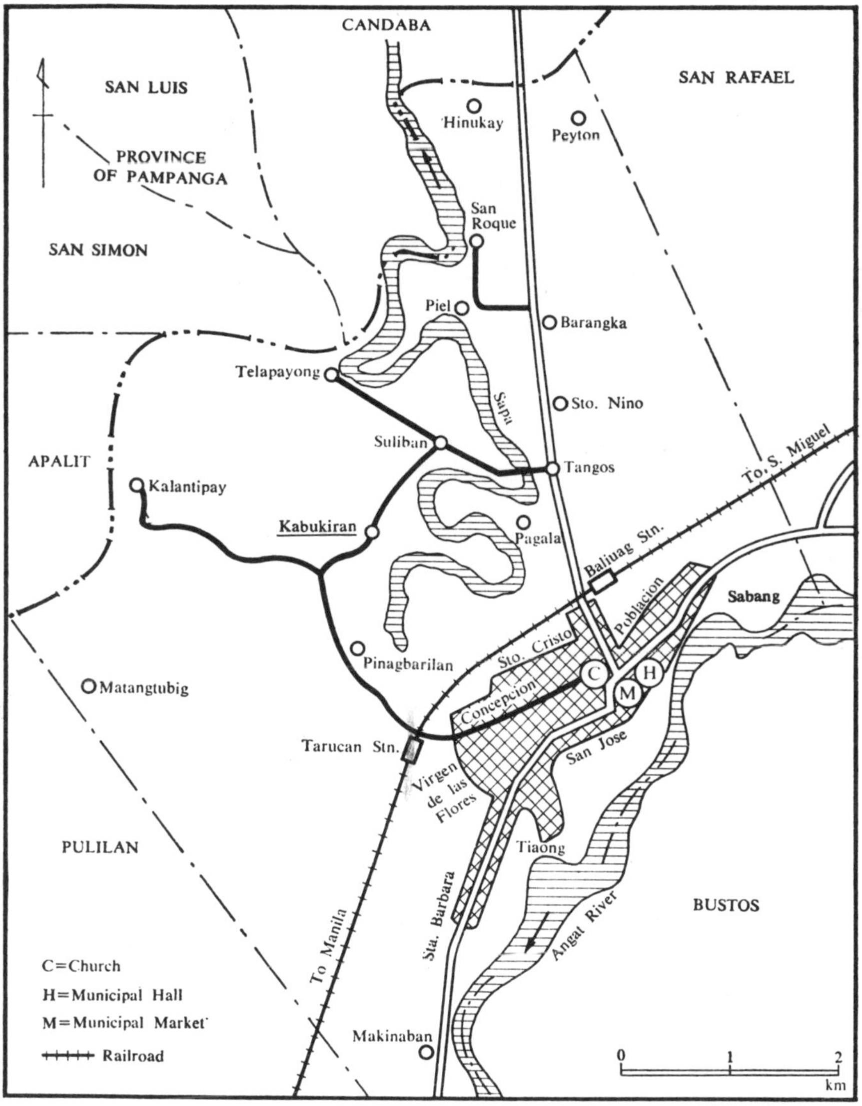

two barrios were divided, and their number stood at 20 in 1964.

Six barrios are clustered along the national highway, forming the town-proper called *kalsada* or *bayan*[3] in which 21,000 population were concentrated in 1960. In three of the six barrios, however, the proportion of farming households is high. In the midst of the *kalsada,* just in front of the church, there is an open space called plaza. This plaza is surrounded by the municipal hall, a municipal market, three banks, three movie theaters, a bus station, and many stores. The plaza also serves as the terminal for small buses and horse carriages, and as a pedicab stand. The central part of *kalsada* is called *poblacion,* and this is the center of marketing in the northern part of the Province of Bulacan. On market days, Wednesday and Saturday, not only inhabitants of Baliuag but people from neighboring municipalities and the Provinces of Pampanga and Nueva Ecija as well throng the *poblacion.* There are a number of rice mills in the municipality and they are the only factories to speak of, even today. Cottage industries, especially *buntal* hat weaving begun in the nineteenth century,[4] and manufacturing of ready-made garments

Table 3.   Farms in Baliuag (1960)

Number of farms	1,537
Total area of farms	3,695.7 ha.
Cultivated land	3,647.5 ha.
Average size of farms	2.4 ha.
Number of farms by size	
under 1.0 ha.	38
1.0 and under 2.0 ha.	583
2.0 and under 3.0 ha.	563
3.0 and under 5.0 ha.	278
5.0 and under 10.0 ha.	49
10.0 and under 20.0 ha.	25
20.0 and under 100.0 ha.	1
Number of farms by tenure	
Full owners	81
Part-owners	16
Tenants	1,436
Managers & others	4

Source: Census of the Philippines, 1960

[3]*Kalsada* means street, and *bayan* town or nation.

and furniture, are flourishing. The municipality has four high schools and one junior college; hence, it is the center of education in the northern part of the Province of Bulacan.

The other 14 barrios are scattered in flat paddy fields lying between the Angat River and the Candaba Swamp.

The 1960 census shows that the total area of the municipality is 4,505 hectares, the farm area 3,695 hectares, and the number of farms 1,537 (Table 3). Almost the whole area of the municipality is covered by the Angat River Irrigation System. Palay is the most important crop grown in the area. Aside from palay, corn, beans, and fruit are grown on a very small scale. Sugarcane and coconut are not grown (Table 4). The fact that the ratio of the gross planted area of palay to the total cultivated land was 177 per cent in 1960 indicates the wide prevalence of double-cropping. The average size of farms is small, with three-fourths of the farming households cultivating one to three hectares of land. The break-down of farming households by tenure shows that tenant farms account for as high as 93.4 per cent of the total farms while the combined total of full owners and part-owners account for only 6.3 per cent. The high ratio of tenant farms in Baliuag compared with other area is revealed through **Map 3**.

Table 4. Principal Crops in Baliuag (1960)

	Area planted	Under irrigation
Palay		
Total	6,445.2 ha.	
First crop lowland	3,537.8	3,457.9 ha.
Second crop lowland	2,902.9	2,888.2
Upland & kaingin*	4.5	
Corn	37.3	
Stringbeans	15.9	
Mango	45.1	
Other fruits	9.2	
Sugarcane	—	
Tobacco	—	
Coconut	—	

* See Appendix B.
Source: Census of the Philippines, 1960

[4]Feodor Jagor described that delicate cigar-case called *petaca* also was famous product of Baliuag in mid-nineteenth century (*Travels in the Philippines* [London, 1875], p.61).

Map 3.   Percentage of Tenant Farms in the Southern Part of Central Luzon (1960)

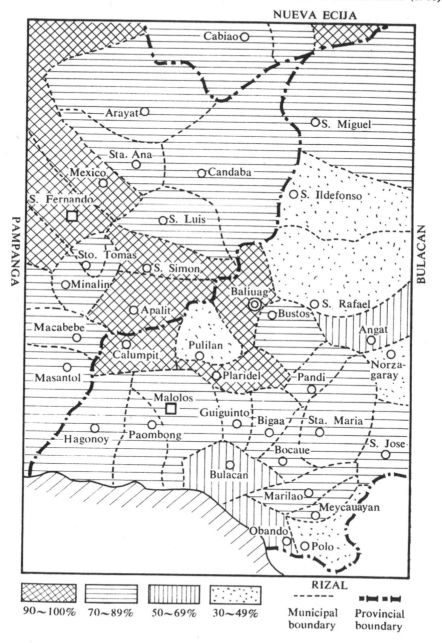

PART II
BARRIO KABUKIRAN, 1963-64

CHAPTER III

The Setting

1. Environment and Life

The barrio which is the subject of this monograph and which shall be referred to as Barrio Kabukiran, is located about 3.5 kilometers northwest of the *poblacion* of Baliuag. Forming a rectangle whose side is about 1.5 kilometers, it is about 151 hectares in area as measured by the writer (Maps 2 and 4). The topography is completely flat, the altitude being only 15 meters above the sea level. In the east section of the village a *sapa* or brook[1] meanders north, while Lateral-D, branching away from the North Main Canal of the Angat River Irrigation System (ARIS), traverses the village from southwest to north. In the middle of the village there is a *bana* or marsh from which the real name of the village is said to have been derived. This *bana* is used for fishing during the slack season, and partly for farming in the rainy season. The soil is classified as Bigaa Clay Loam.

The climate of the area belongs to the climatic type generalized in the west coast of the Philippines; that is, there are distinct dry and rainy seasons. In June the western monsoon called *habagat* begins to blow and the rainy season sets in. About 90 per cent of the annual rainfall is concentrated in the period from June to September, during which time typhoons frequently cause damage. In October the rain begins to diminish, and from January on there is no rainfall at all, ushering in cool, dry days. The period from March to May is the hottest season of the year with no rainfall. Since there is no observation post in the municipality, data

---

[1]This brook flows north into the Candaba Swamp and is used as drainage for the paddy fields.

Map 4. Outline of Barrio Kabukiran

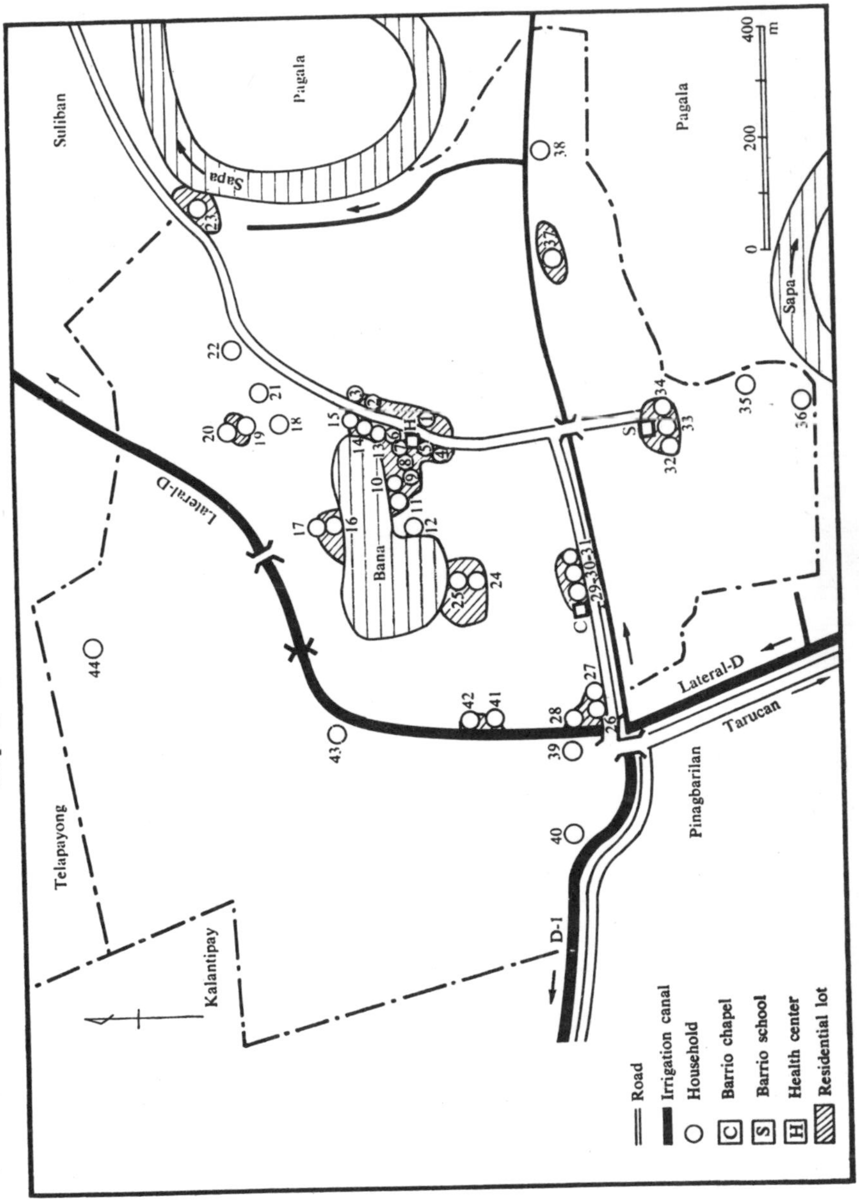

Table 5.   Rainfall in Bustos (1963–64)

Period	mm
May 1963	35.6
June	657.1
July	276.9
August	220.9
September	476.1
October	68.3
November	35.3
December	56.7
January 1964	—
February	—
March	—
April	—
Total	1,826.9

Remarks: Observed at Bustos Dam
Source: ARIS office

on the rainfall in the neighboring Municipality of Bustos as recorded at the dam site of ARIS are given in Table 5 for reference. The rainfall in Kabukiran could be estimated at about 1,800 millimeters a year.

There are two routes from the *poblacion* to Kabukiran. One goes north along Candaba Road, turns west at Tangos to Telapayong Road, and turns southwest at Barrio Suliban; the other route, starting from Tarucan Station on the western edge of the *kalsada,* takes Kalantipay Road along Lateral-D, and reaches the western tip of the village. Either route is about five kilometers. Pedicabs are the most common means of transportation in the *kalsada,* and "jeepneys", remodeled jeeps, are used as small buses running between the *kalsada* and distant barrios, while one-horse carriages called *karitela* ply between the plaza in the *poblacion* and nearby barrios such as Kabukiran several times a day. There are five bicycles in the village.

Barrio Kabukiran was not mentioned in the census report of 1918. It appeared for the first time in census of 1939 with a population of 520, and then with 539 in 1948. According to the 1960 census, the population was 423, of which 222 were males and 203 females. The survey by this writer, however, indicated that the population of the village as of April 1964 was 228 (123 males and 105 females) and the number of permanent households was 44. Since in the province there are only 30 barrios whose population is less than 300, Kabukiran is small in size. The difference in the population between the 1960 census and the 1964 survey was not due to emigration, but to the fact that the 1960 census figure was padded (see Sec. 3 of this chapter). During World War II and the Huk disturbance the number of households in the village decreased considerably for people sought refuge in the *kalsada*. In the late 1950's many returned to the village. The number of households, however, is always changing, for instance, at the outset of the present survey two households left the village.

In general, both agglomerated and dispersed patterns of settlement are observed in Central Luzon. Here in Kabukiran the dispersed pattern is found (Map 4). Out of the total 44 households in the village, 15 are clustered in the middle of the village; the only *sarisari,* or small general store, in the village and a small concrete-block building, which is called the Health Center,[2] are also located in the middle. Other houses, grouped in twos or threes, are scattered in the paddy fields here and there. Not a few are standing alone, isolated from others. Nineteen houses are surrounded by groves of trees, while the other houses are bare of trees or have a few clumps of bamboo around them. Since the houses are very simple in structure, it is not uncommon to move them to other sites without disassembling. Three such cases were observed during the survey.

The only road in the village is the one connecting Telapayong Road with Kalantipay Road. During the rainy season this road gets so muddy that it becomes inaccessible to vehicles. Only 19 houses stand facing the road; those who live in other houses must take footpaths on ridgeways between paddy fields or on the embankments of the irrigation canal. There are three concrete bridges spanning the canals in the village. Aside from these bridges, one must cross the watercourses on bamboo poles. However, conditions of transportation in Kabukiran are rather favorable compared with other villages. There are many villages in this area that have no road at all.

As for public facilities in the village, there are the Health Center mentioned above, a barrio school, and a *bisita* or Catholic chapel. There is no electricity, nor other utilities.

The survey by the writer shows that the total area of cultivated land

[2]A Rural Health Unit is supposed to visit the village occasionally, although the writer never saw such a visit. But weekly medical service is rendered by a Rural Health Unit consisting of a doctor, two nurses and a midwife at the Health Center of neighboring Barrio Telapayong which is two kilometers away.

in the village is 134 hectares.[3] This means some 90 per cent of the village land is cultivated. According to the 1960 census, the ratio of cultivated land to total area in the Municipality of Baliuag as a whole was 81 per cent, and the figure in Kabukiran may be regarded as average. The rest of the land is used as residential land, roads, and watercourses, and there is no grass land nor forest. There are few dry fields in the village, and vegetables are grown in *bakuran,* or backyard, or in paddy fields when palay is not being grown; therefore, almost all farmland in Kabukiran is actually utilized as paddy fields.

Irrigation is well developed in the village, for a lateral of the Angat River Irrigation System cuts across the village and numbers of ditches called *kanal* and *sanga* branch away from the lateral. Both due to the relief of the land surface by 15 to 40 centimeters and due to the distance from watercourses, some parts of farmland cannot be irrigated. The area of such unirrigated paddy fields and the *bana,* or marsh, is about 10 hectares, which remains as single-crop land.

The possibility of harvesting two crops a year depends on the availability of irrigation water. Nearly all paddy fields on the north side of Lateral-D are double-crop land, whereas on the south side of the Lateral-D single-crop land is interwoven with double-crop land because of the slight relief (Map 5). The area of double-crop land is 78.7 hectares, and that of single-crop land in total is 55.4 hectares; the ratio of double-crop land to all cultivated land is therefore 59 per cent. It should be noted that even in this region where the irrigation system is best developed of any region in the Philippines, double-cropping of palay is not necessarily widespread (see Chap. V, Sec. 2).

The utilization of *bakuran,* that is, backyards for vegetable and/or fruit, is not advanced in this village nor in most of the barrios of the Municipality of Baliuag, as compared with other municipalities like Malolos or Guiguinto. The number of fruit trees in the village is small, only 15 mango trees. Vegetables are grown only for home consumption. Very little effort is made to raise chickens or hogs.

Regarding housing, there are only nine houses made of wood, and in only two houses is concrete used as a building material. Ordinary houses with bamboo floors and walls are stilted on bamboo poles, and roofs are thatched with nipa. These houses have no glass windows; windows are

---

[3]It was impossible to obtain the exact area of farmland through interviews with villagers alone. This writer attempted to obtain an accurate figure by combining the results of several interviews with each cultivator with his own measurements in the field.

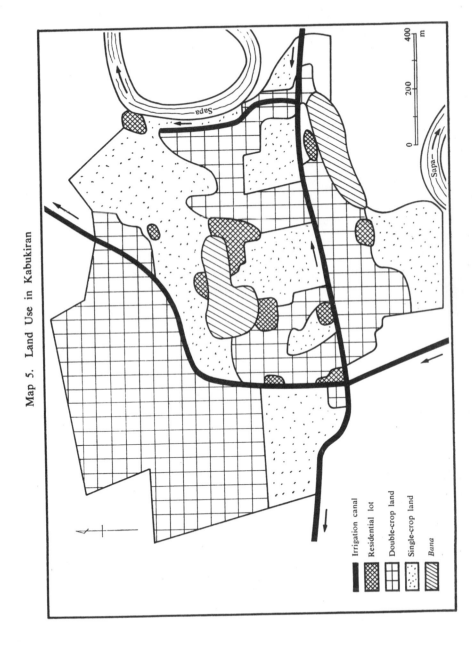

Map 5. Land Use in Kabukiran

Irrigation canal
Residential lot
Double-crop land
Single-crop land
Bana

made of nipa flaps. The houses have only one or two rooms, and many houses are bare of furniture. Only four households own ready-made wooden chairs; the others have home-made bamboo or wooden benches. Those who use beds are exceptional; in ordinary households they sleep on *banig,* or *buri* leaf mats, unfolded on the floor, wrapping themselves with blankets or cotton sheets. Many houses are not attached with out-houses. In the kitchen there are usually a few stones so arranged that they serve for cooking. The space under the floor of the house, called *silong,* is sometimes as much as two meters high, and is used for storage of farm implements or as pens for domestic animals. Typical plans of houses are shown in Fig. 1.

Since there is no electricity, oil lamps are commonly used for lighting, but a few households use "Coleman lamps" of the incandescent type. The level of underground water is high, and it is not difficult to obtain water by the use of hand-pumps, which are owned by many households. For laundering, both well water and canal water is used.

Villagers have three meals a day, and their staple food is rice. Side dishes[4] are of poor quality, however. The most common side dish is a salty soup containing leaves of a water grass called *kangkong,* which grows in paddy fields. For seasoning, vinegar and salt commonly are used. Meals are regarded as very substantial when they are accompanied by dried fishes or by catfish caught in the nearby pond. Chicken, pork, and other meats or fresh fishes sometimes can be purchased at the market, but they are very rarely served.

Transistor radios are owned by only seven households, and no household subscribes to a newspaper. News heard at the market is brought back to the village and circulated among villagers; communication by word of mouth is the major source of information. Mail is delivered to the village by a villager who works at the municipal hall when he returns home. There are no amusement facilities. Except on festival days, this writer has never seen the villagers play with a ball. A few people own guitars. Some of the young people go to movie theaters in the *poblacion,* but most villagers spend their leisure getting together in front of the *sarisari* store or sitting on the roadside and chatting. Though many Filipino farmers are enthusiastic about cock-fighting, no villager in Kabukiran raises fighting cocks.

---

[4]In Southeast Asian Countries cooked rice is supposed to be main dish, while meat, fish, vegetable, soup and other foods are considered as side dish or subsidiary food.

Fig. 1.   Plans of Farmhouses

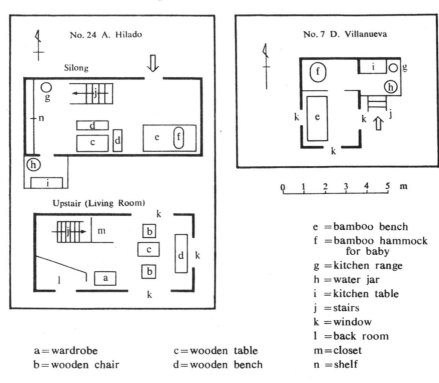

a = wardrobe

b = wooden chair

c = wooden table

d = wooden bench

e = bamboo bench

f = bamboo hammock for baby

g = kitchen range

h = water jar

i = kitchen table

j = stairs

k = window

l = back room

m = closet

n = shelf

	A. Hilado (No. 24)	D. Villanueva (No. 7)
Materials		
Roof	Sheet zinc	Nipa
Exterior wall	Living room—wood *Silong*—Bamboo	Nipa and bamboo
Interior wall	Plywood	Bamboo split
Floor	Living room—wood *Silong*—earth	Bamboo split
Window	Wooden sash inlayed with *kapis* shells	Nipa flap
Ready-made furniture	Five pieces including a wardrobe.	None
Size of household		
Farming season	11	5
Slack season	9	5

The language spoken in the village is Tagalog. Although most villagers have been taught English in primary school, English is never spoken in daily life, even on official occasions.

The standard of education in the Philippines is rather high compared with other Asian countries. In the Municipality of Baliuag 15 out of the 20 barrios have their own primary or elementary schools. Ten are elementary schools with six grades, while the rest are primary schools of up to Grade 4. Three of these 15 schools have only one classroom. The barrio school in Kabukiran is one of these one-room primary schools. The number of pupils in June 1964 was 64 in total; 32 in Grade 1, 12 in Grade 3 and 20 in Grade 4. Eighteen pupils were from neighboring barrios.[5] Children of Grade 5 and 6 have to go to the elementary school in Barrio Concepcion 2.5 kilometers away. Primary school is compulsory in this country, but the rate of school attendance is rather low, usually about 70 per cent.

In 1964, there is only a school mistress commuting from the *kalsada,* and she is not concerned with the village life. The level of schooling of the villagers is mostly up to primary course, but there are seven high school graduates, three of them being heads of households. At present, four are attending high school.

This writer's impression, confirmed by government officials and a Filipino rural sociologist, was that, as a village in Central Luzon, the habitants of Kabukiran enjoy a lower-than-average standard of living.

2.   Historical Background

It is extremely difficult to trace back the history of Barrio Kabukiran. Historical documents are not available at all, and even through interviewing villagers it is difficult to certify events before World War II. It has proved impossible to retrace to the 1910's, which is, in this writer's opinion, an important epoch in the economic history of the Philippines; not to speak of the mid-nineteenth century, during which time the prototype of the land system in Central Luzon is believed to have been formed.

Kabukiran is rather a new barrio. The Cadastral Survey in 1926 showed that this area was divided between three barrios, Santo Cristo,

---

[5]Pupils of a barrio school are not always from that barrio. In this school year, Grade 2 is not organized in the barrio school of Kabukiran, so that children of Grade 2 have to go to a neighboring barrio school, while children of barrios where one of the grades was not organized may come to the school in Kabukiran.

Telapayong, and Matangtubig; even today the land registration is recorded not only as Kabukiran, but as parts of Telapayong, Pagala, and Pinag-barilan.

It is not known when people began to inhabit the village. It is believed that in neighboring Telapayong and Matangtubig settlements developed earlier than in Kabukiran. The number of farming households in Kabukiran in the early twentieth century is said to have been less than 10. The breakdown of the present 44 households by the generation during which they settled in the village is as follows:[6] generations before grandfathers, four; generation of grandfathers, nine; generation of fathers, 16; generation of present household heads, 15. The 31 households which settled in the village during the generation of fathers and present householders are broken down by the time of their settlement as follows: before 1925, five; 1926-45, 15; and after 1946, 11. In other words, 57 per cent of the households settled in the village after the irrigation project was completed 40 years ago, and 25 per cent migrated to the village from nearby barrios after World War II.

The construction of the Angat River Irrigation System between 1922 and 1926 was an epoch-making event in the history of the village. Until that time the land lying between the Angat River and the Candaba Swamp was mainly devoted to cultivation of sugarcane. The sugar industry at that time remained at the stage of producing *panocha* and *muscovado*,[7] and small *muscovado* mills existed in Telapayong and other nearby barrios. When the modern centrals (large scale centrifugal sugar mills) in Central Luzon were established successively in the late 1910's and in the 1920's, this area was left behind.[8] Just at the time when long distances from centrals were putting the growing of cane in the area at a disadvantage, the irrigation project was completed. With irrigation water now available, the paddy fields were opened and palay was grown instead of

---

[6]The period of evacuation to the *kalsada* from the 1940's to the early 1950's is left out of this account.

[7]*Panocha* is a sort of crude sugar obtained through the most primitive method of pressing cane by *kalabaw* (water buffalo) and boiling the juice in an open pot. This kind of sugar-making is done by peasants as side work. *Muscovado* is raw sugar obtained by first squeezing the juice from cane by steam-driven rollers and then boiling the juice in a sequence of pots. This kind of processing was common at small mills in sugar estates.

[8]From the year 1919 to 1929, 10 centrals were established in Central Luzon, that is, four in Pampanga, three in Tarlac, one each in Nueva Ecija, Bulacan (at the Municipality of Calumpit) and Pangasinan. Out of these 10, two centrals in Pampanga, two in Tarlac and one in Pangasinan are still being operated. The rest were closed during World War II.

cane.[9] Thus the pattern of land use as it exists today was formed by the mid-1930's.[10]

Changes during the period as suggested by census figures are given in Table 6. Since statistical bases varied from year to year, it is somewhat problematical to make a comparison without adjusting figures. Nevertheless, the figures suggest that the ratio of irrigated land in Baliuag increased from 14 per cent in 1918 to 48 per cent in 1939 along with a sharp decline in cane land. A farmer who migrated to Kabukiran from a neighboring village in 1934 recalls that since there was a shortage of cultivators at that time anyone could easily rent land from landlords on a share basis. Changes in farm management due to the opening of paddy fields are believed to have caused changes in land tenure.

In this way the village became part of the rice-growing region with land tenure based on a share tenancy system in the last half of the 1930's. However, the heavy pressure of the landlords on the tenants resulted in the tenants' movement which was centered in the southern part of the Central Luzon Plain.[11] During World War II this area became a stronghold of the Hukbalahap resistance movement. After independence the Hukbalahap launched an armed struggle against the government of the Republic and this area, being close to Mt. Arayat and the Candaba

Table 6. Changes in Irrigated Land and Sugarcane Land in Baliuag (1918-60)

| Census Year | Baliuag | | | | | Province of Bulacan |
	Number of farms	Area of farms	Cultivated land	Irrigated land	Area planted to sugarcane	Area planted to sugarcane
1918	1,790	2,855 ha.	2,424 ha.	401 ha.	n.a.	3,928 ha.
1939	1,775	4,054	3,884	1,955	10 ha.	1,524
1948	1,342	2,736	2,610	2,093	0	607
1960	1,537	3,695	3,646	3,457	—	533

Source: Census of the Philippines, 1918, 1939, 1948 and 1960.

[9]Similar change was observed in Paombong, Bulacan. Sugarcane land was converted to paddy field by the construction of irrigation canals in 1926. (Charles Kaut, "The Principle of Contingency in Tagalog Society," *Asian Studies,* III [1965], 10.)

[10]A rough road was opened at the time. Before that people walked on footpaths between paddy fields when going to the *kalsada.*

[11]TAKAHASHI, "Firippin no tochi kaikaku (Land Reform in the Philippines)," in *Ajia no tochi kaikaku* (Land Reforms in Asia), ed. OWADA Keiki (Tokyo, 1962), pp. 311-321.

Swamp, was the scene of heavy fighting. Referring to the period between 1947 and 1949, people say, "From morning to three in the afternoon the government forces ruled, and from 4 p.m. on the Hukbalahap ruled." Many villagers moved to the *kalsada* to avoid fighting and came to the farms to work only in the daytime. Only seven households stayed in the village in those years.

As the disturbance ceased in the early 1950's, the villagers returned to the village in an increasing number, and at the same time two-crop-a-year farming was introduced in the village. Rivera and McMillan say that on the regional level rents paid by tenants decreased in those years due to the Hukbalahap pressures.[12] It is possible to recognize that, in Kabukiran too, rents were somewhat reduced during the Hukbalahap uprisings, as well as after the legislation of the Agricultural Tenancy Act under President Magsaysay.

We have seen already that the name of Barrio Kabukiran was listed in the census of 1939 and from then onwards, but it is said the status of the barrio was as a *sitio* or sub-village of Barrio Telapayong. In 1955 the villagers built a *bisita,* or chapel, of their own and the barrio obtained full status. The circumstances under which the new status was obtained are not very well known; but villagers attribute the reasons for the new status to the increase in population and the distance between Kabukiran and Telapayong. In 1958 Telapayong Road and Kalantipay Road were improved, and in 1959 a path connecting the village to the two roads was converted into a vehicular road, thus enabling automobiles and *karitela* to come to the village.

3.   Population and Occupations

To obtain the exact population and number of households was not easy in this village. As was mentioned in Section 1, the population was 425 according to the 1960 census. Although the number of households was not given in the census, it would be around 73 if we assume that the average size of households was the same as in the Municipality of Baliuag (5.8). Villagers, however, gave many different answers in this regard; their figures ranged from 50 to 70. The first reason for the variance in figures was the large number of cultivators who live outside the village but do farming inside the village (Chap. V, Sec. 1). Such cultivators include former villagers who left the village during the war or the unrest

[12]*Central Luzon,* p. 60.

but still continue to commute to the village for farming. The number of the former is 31, and that of the latter is eight. The second reason is the ambiguity in barrio boundaries and the wide dispersion of settlement. Villagers maintain that those who live near the boundaries belong to Kabukiran, though some of the latter say that they belong to other barrios. The third reason is the padding of population figures in making official reports. It is said that the fact of a population exceeding 500 was claimed as a ground for the complete separation from Telapayong.[13] Since then the population figure in official reports has been padded by counting as villagers those who do not live, but do farming, in the village, and those who shifted to the *kalsada*.

In this survey villagers are defined as those who live in the village on a permanent basis and regard themselves as villagers of Kabukiran; and those who own dwellings both in the village and in the *kalsada* but whose subsistence is based in the village rather than the *kalsada*. Thus 44 households were confirmed as members of village community as of April 1964 and the population was 228 including unmarried family members who were away from home but still shared in family accounts.

The breakdown of the population by sex and age is given in Fig. 2. The male/female ratio is 100 : 85, though in the Philippine rural areas

Fig. 2. Age Distribution in Kabukiran (1964)

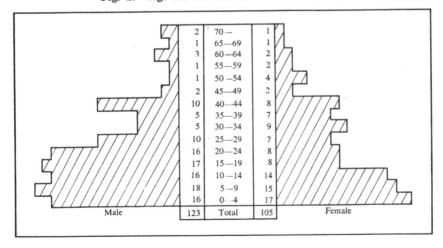

Male	2	70 —	1	Female
	1	65—69	1	
	3	60—64	2	
	1	55—59	2	
	1	50—54	4	
	2	45—49	2	
	10	40—44	8	
	5	35—39	7	
	5	30—34	9	
	10	25—29	7	
	16	20—24	8	
	17	15—19	8	
	16	10—14	14	
	18	5—9	15	
	16	0—4	17	
Male	123	Total	105	Female

[13]This information was given by a former vice-mayor. The Barrio Charter of 1959 (Republic Act No. 2370) prescribes "All barrio existing at the time of the passage of this Act shall come under the provisions here of . . . no new barrios may be created if its population is less than five hundred persons." (Sec. 3)

females generally are predominant. It is one of the demographic characteristics of the Philippines that the percentage of the labor force, or the
productive age group, in total population is comparatively low. In Kabukiran, however, the number of the population 14 years old and under or
65 years old and over is 101, while the population between 15 and 64
years of age numbers 127, with the former being 44 per cent of total
population. This is because the number of people 65 years old and over
is only five. Most of those who moved to the *kalsada* during the Huk
uprisings returned to the village when peace was restored, but many old
people who had retired from productive work remained there. The number of men in the 25-39 age bracket is small due to emigration, while
a majority of young people of 25 years old and under stay in the village
and help the heads of households with farming or are engaged in agricultural, or other, wage labor. Out-migration increases in the 25-30 age
bracket and older age bracket. This phenomenon is believed to be related
to the fact that men are most marriageable when they are between 22
and 25 years of age.

Next, let us examine the occupations of the villagers (Table 7). Out
of the 44 households, 36 are farming[14] households. All the farming households are tenant farmers, but they also are engaged in non-farming work,
more or less. The heads of nine farming households are engaged pri-

Table 7. Households by Occupation (1964)

Farming households	36
Occupation of head of household other than farming	
Karitela drivers	5
Pedicab drivers	2
Barber	1
Municipal clerk	1
Carpenters	5
Agricultural laborers	19
None	3
Non-farming households	8
Agricultural laborers	5
Tractor driver	1
Unemployed	2
Total	44

Source: Field survey by the author.

[14]Here in this monograph, farming means the cultivation of one's own holding.

marily in non-farming work rather than in farming, with eight of them self-employed in services, i.e., five *karitela* drivers, two pedicab drivers, one barber (his wife keeps a *sarisari* store). The ninth one is a public servant working at the municipal hall. On the other hand, the number of non-farming households is eight or 18 per cent of the total. The heads of five of these households are agricultural laborers; one is a tractor driver; and two are unemployed (one is a household of two old women, and the other a retired old man).

Since employment structure is dealt with in detail in Chapter IX, here we shall examine the occupational composition of the population only briefly (Table 8).

The number of employed persons is 109. If we count as non-farmers those heads of farming households who are engaged primarily in non-farming work, the number of farmers is only 32. There are 21 other self-employed workers. On the other hand, there are 56 agricultural and non-agricultural wage workers. Non-agricultural workers include wire-

Table 8. Employed Persons by Occupation (1964)

		Male	Female	Total
Self-employed	Farmers	32	—	32
	Karitela drivers	7	—	7
	Pedicab drivers	3	—	3
	Barber	1	—	1
	Sarisari store keeper and cantina* keeper	—	2	2
	Buntal hat weavers**	—	8	8
Employed	Agricultural laborers	20	25	45
	Municipal clerk	1	—	1
	Tractor driver	1	—	1
	Wireman	1	—	1
	Sawmill worker	1	—	1
	Automobile repairmen	3	—	3
	Store clerks and beautician's apprentice	—	3	3
	Seamstress	—	1	1
Total		70	39	109

* See Appendix B.

** Those who weave more than one hat a week and have no other jobs.

Source: Field survey by the author.

man, tractor driver, sawmill worker, store clerk, beautician's apprentice, and five persons who work in Manila as automobile repairman, seamstress, and store clerk. Thirty-nine out of 109 workers are women.[15] Generally speaking, Philippine housewives are engaged only in domestic work and not in farm work; the writer has seldom seen housewives in Kabukiran helping their husbands on the farms. During the busiest farming season, however, 25 women in the village including 15 housewives are employed as agricultural laborers. Since *buntal* hat weaving is one of the most important cottage industries in the region, almost all women in the village are engaged in this work. But only those who weave more than one hat a week are counted as hat weavers.

[15]One of the characteristics of the labor structure in the Philippines is that labor force participation rate for females is comparatively high. In May 1964, the proportion of the population 10 years old and over in the labor force to the total population was 78.2 per cent for males and 42.0 per cent for females, and the female labor force accounted for 35.3 per cent of the total labor force. (*Philippine Statistical Survey of Households Bulletin, Labor Force Data, May, 1964,* Series No. 17, [1965].)

CHAPTER IV

Landownership

1. The Scale of Holdings

The cadastral survey in this region was completed in 1926, and land titles are registered with the provincial government in Malolos. Cadastral documents, such as "Declaration of Real Property" and "Real Property Tax Register," also are kept at the municipal hall. Officials at municipal offices and government agencies report that there are no large-scale landlords in this region. However, such statements appear to reflect the fact that since many landlords own land in several municipalities, information on the actual situation of landownership is difficult to obtain. Data available at the ARIS office in the Municipality of Plaridel, for example, indicate that 28,751 hectares of land in the ARIS district, divided into 15,111 lots, are owned by an aggregate number of 11,184 landlords. But information on the exact number and size of landlords is not available.

This writer, therefore, integrated the areas of lots held by individual landowners by examining the ledger book for collection of irrigation fees at the ARIS office. By this calculation data were obtained on landowners

Table 9. Landowners Owning 40 Hectares and
More in the ARIS District (1953, 1964)

Size (ha.)	1953	1964
700 and more	1	1
500 and under 700	—	—
300 and under 500	1	1
200 and under 300	1	1
100 and under 200	10	10
50 and under 100	9	8
40 and under 50	4	4
Total	26	25
Total area of land owned	3,614.2 ha.	3,526.6 ha.

Source: Integrated from the ledger book for collection of irrigation fees at the ARIS office.

who own more than 40 hectares of land in the ARIS district (Table 9). The list is headed by Perfecto Cruz of Pulilan, Bulacan (706 hectares), followed by Aurea Escaler of Apalit, Pampanga (351 hectares), and the Rustia brothers of Baliuag (296 hectares), and there are 25 landlords who own more than 40 hectares of land. The total acreage of land owned by these 25 landlords is 3,526 hectares, or 12 per cent of land in the ARIS district. It can be assumed that these landlords are actually bigger than suggested by Table 9, because the ledger book lists only irrigated land, and chances are that many of them own land outside the ARIS district. Besides, there exists a large amount of Church land[1] (*kapilya* or *mitra*[2]) in this region, but the exact figures cannot be obtained because these are registered not only in the name of the Church but often in the names of *namumuisan* or *arrendadors*.[3]

The large-scale landlords with more than 40 hectares of land in the ARIS district who own land in the Municipality of Baliuag are given in Table 10. The total area of land owned by these eight landlords in Baliuag is 425 hectares. In addition, the Church owns at least 134.5 hectares in Barrio Suliban and Barrio Telapayong and 21 hectares in Barrio Santo Niño. All told, the nine landlords own at least 580 hectares of land. According to the official tabulation by ARIS office, the number of owners of irrigated land in Baliuag is 871, and their holdings total 3,444 hectares.[4] Therefore, at least 17 per cent of the total irrigated land in Baliuag is held by these nine landowners.

The history of these large-scale holdings are not well known, although many of them are supposed to have been formed in the old days. It is said that the previous generations of the Rustias and the Ponces[5] owned

[1]The noted friar estate, Buenavista Estate, northeast of Baliuag, was founded in 1862 on the royal grand by Queen Isabella to the San Juan de Dios Hospital, Manila. Its 27,408 hectares of land stretching into the Municipalities of San Ildefonso, San Rafael and Bustos was redistributed by the Commonwealth Government after 1939. (*Balak na Tuwirang Pagbibili ng Asienda Buenavista* [n.p., 1941]. James S. Allen, "Agrarian Tendencies in the Philippines," *Pacific Affairs*, XI [1938], 54.) Several Church estates such as Bahay Pare Estate, north of Baliuag, were also redistributed, but Church estates still remain in many places.

[2]*Kapilya* and mitra originally meant chapel and bishopric respectively, but in this region they mean Church-owned land.

[3]*Namumuisan* and *arrendador* acquire rights to manage land for fixed fees, and collect rents from tenant farmers. They are intermediary landlords rather than managers. See Chapter VII.

[4]"Management and Operation of Irrigation and Drainage Systems in the Philippines," presented at the Irrigation Symposium of the Bureau of Public Works, Manila, August 1963, (mimeographed).

[5]This family produced Mariano Ponce, one of the prominent leaders in the Philippine Revolution toward the end of the nineteenth century.

Table 10. Landowners Owning Land in Baliuag among Those Owning
40 Hectares and More in the ARIS District (1964)

Name of landowners	Address	Land owned in the ARIS district	Land owned in Baliuag
1. Emilio Rustia	Baliuag	246.54 ha.	92.73 ha.
2. Jose Rustia	Baliuag	49.06	49.06
3. Gerfurdes Cruz	Baliuag	98.76	82.54
4. Benito Dionicio	Baliuag	57.17	55.51
5. Mary G. Ponce	Baliuag	75.27	64.78
6. Pereglina Tan	Manila	88.70	62.84
7. Perfecto Cruz	Pulilan	705.87	10.35
8. Hermogenes Reyes	Malolos	81.41	6.52
Total		1,402.78	424.33
9. Roman Catholic Church	Manila	n.a.	155.6
Grand total			579.9

Remarks: The amount of land owned by the Roman Catholic Church was
calculated by adding the figure in the ledger book to the data
obtained in interviews.
Source: Same as Table 9.

more than 400 hectares of land, but their estates were divided into smaller
plots by inheritance. Both the Rustias and the Ponces own large man-
sions, and operate such businesses as rice mills, tractors and *telyadora*
for hire, in Baliuag. They delegate the management of their land to
katiwala,[6] and members of the families usually live in Manila engaged in
such professions as medicine or law. It is said that they tend to convert
their farmland to real estate in Manila.

Now, let us examine landownership in Barrio Kabukiran. Regarding
this village the cadastral data are quite complicated and difficult to obtain,
because the lot number is arranged not only as Kabukiran, but as the
parts of three barrios, i.e., Pagala, Telapayong and Pinagbarilan. So data
were gathered through interviews with each household, and then confirmed by the ledger book of ARIS. The area of farmland in the village
thus obtained is 135 hectares, and the number of landowners is 25 (Table
11). The size of land owned ranges from 0.5 to 20 hectares, but the
majority is between one and four hectares. Out of the 25 landowners,
13 live in Baliuag and 12 live outside Baliuag. The average amount of

[6]*Katiwala* is a farm-overseer posted by landlord. See Chapter VII, Section 1.

Table 11.   Owners of Farmland in Kabukiran (1964)

Size	Owners living in Baliuag	Owners living outside Baliuag	Total
20.0 ~ 25.0 ha.	—	1	1
10.0 ~ 19.9	2	1	3
5.0 ~ 9.9	1	3	4
2.0 ~ 4.9	5	6	11
1.0 ~ 1.9	2	1	3
0.5 ~ 0.9	3	—	3
Total	13	12	25
Total land owned	53.1 ha.	82.1 ha.	135.2 ha.
Average size	4.1	6.8	5.4

Source: Field survey by the author.

land owned by those living in Baliuag is 4.1 hectares, and that of land owned by those living outside Baliuag is 6.8 hectares. This type of small-scale landownership is called *lupang Tagalog* (Tagalog land) and distinguished from *lupang hacienda* (estate land) and *lupang kapilya* (Church land).

Since both landownership and relationships between landlords and tenants have been unstable, it is difficult to trace back the history of landownership in the village. Let us take a particular tract of land in the central part of the village as an example. The land is said to have been owned by a Filipina named Maria[7] who lived in the Municipality of Malolos in the early twentieth century. When she died, the land was inherited by her daughter and managed by the daughter's husband, Antonio Ramos, who lived in the Municipality of Calumpit. At that time the size of their land in the village was about 40 hectares. In the early part of 1930's the land, then sugarcane fields, was bought by Jacinto Ponce, a *propiyetaryo* (landlord or man of property) in Baliuag, who began to turn the land into paddy fields. In 1937 Jacinto died and the land was inherited by his nephew, Ramon Ponce, said to be a *propiyetaryo* with no particular job. In 1956 Ramon sold 26 hectares of land to M. Salvador in Quezon City through a real estate agent (*ahente*) in order to meet expenses for his son's study in the United States and for the construction of apartment houses in Manila. The land in question

[7]Her exact name is not known. Villagers remember her as **Mariang Malolos**.

Map 6.   Landowners in Kabukiran

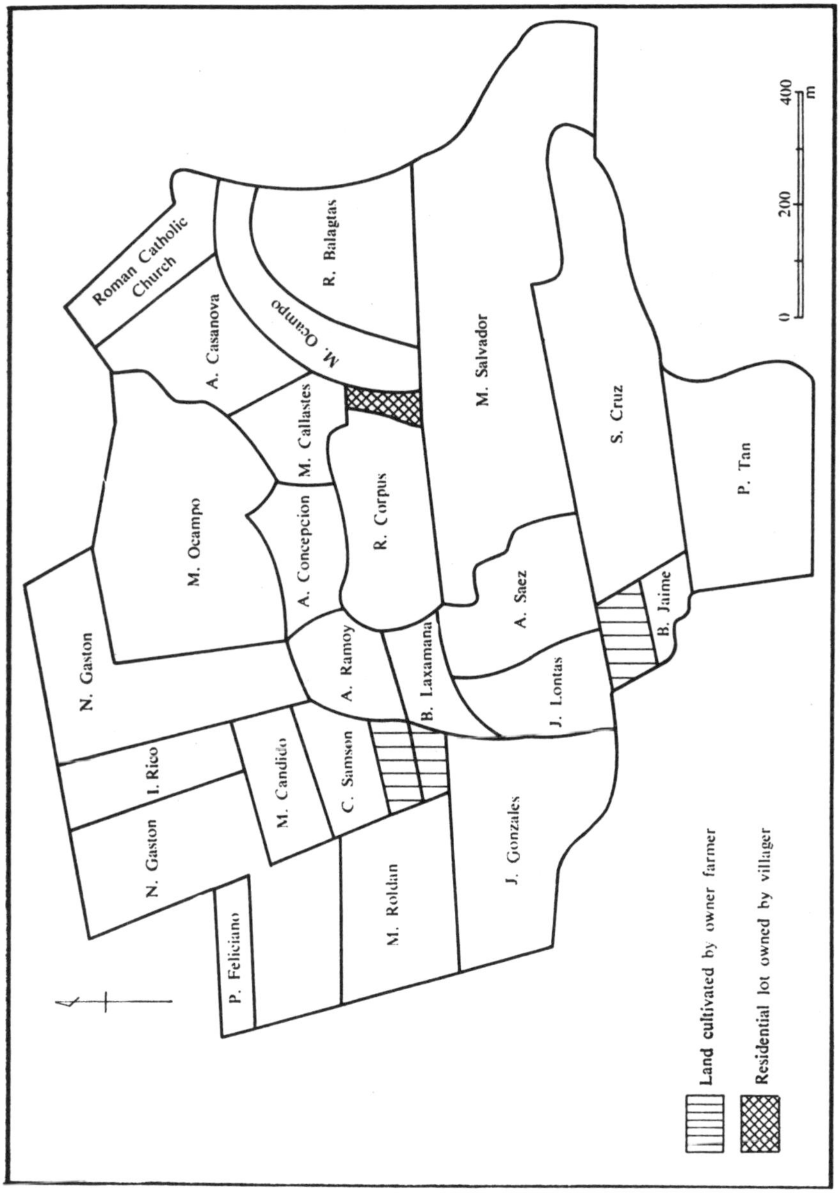

Land cultivated by owner farmer

Residential lot owned by villager

Roman Catholic Church

R. Balagtas

A. Casanova

M. Ocampo

M. Callastes

M. Salvador

A. Concepcion

R. Corpus

S. Cruz

M. Ocampo

N. Gaston

A. Ramoy

B. Laxamana

A. Saez

B. Jaime

P. Tan

I. Rico

M. Candido

C. Samson

J. Lontas

J. Gonzales

N. Gaston

P. Feliciano

M. Roldan

0   200   400

m

changed hands five times in the past 50 years. Such a case is not an exception; thus we can observe fluidity in landownership.

2. Landowners

Out of the 25 landowners in the village, only three are owner farmers, all of whom live outside the village, and one is under joint ownership. The rest are absentee landlords who rent their land to tenant farmers. Sketches of such landowners will be presented here.

(1) The Corpus Family: This is the only landowning family who lives in the village. It owns 3.5 hectares of farmland and 3.0 hectares of residential land in the village, and 5.6 hectares of farmland outside the village, so that the total land held is 12.1 hectares. Although the land

Fig. 3. *Comunidado* of the Corpus Family

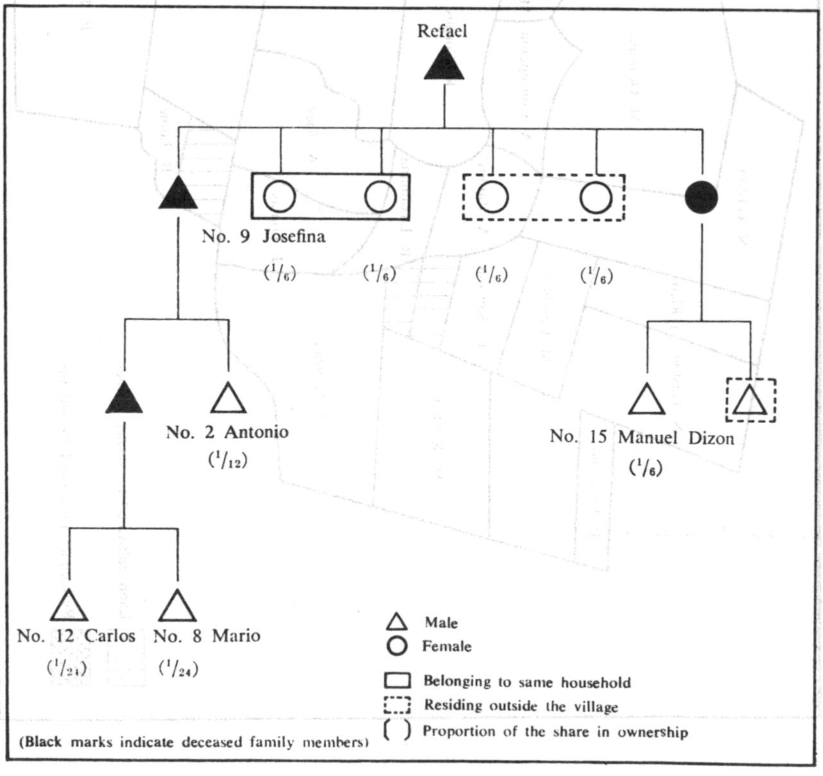

Refael

No. 9 Josefina

$(^1/_6)$ $(^1/_6)$ $(^1/_6)$ $(^1/_6)$

No. 2 Antonio
$(^1/_{12})$

No. 15 Manuel Dizon
$(^1/_6)$

No. 12 Carlos   No. 8 Mario
$(^1/_{24})$ $(^1/_{24})$

△ Male
○ Female

☐ Belonging to same household
⊡ Residing outside the village
( ) Proportion of the share in ownership

(Black marks indicate deceased family members)

is still registered in the name of Rafael Corpus who died in 1954, it was inherited by his six children and jointly owned. When two of his children died, their shares were inherited by their children. Thus, at present the land is jointly owned by eight persons of three generations (Fig. 3). The joint ownership of property resulting from the inheritance system in which the parental legacy is divided equally among siblings is called *comunidado*,[8] and many such cases are found in the area. Out of nine hectares of farmland, 6.5 hectares, including 3.5 hectares of *bana,* are rented and farmed by two nephews, Antonio Corpus (No. 2)[9] and Manuel Dizon (No. 15). The rents for this land (about 120 to 150 cavans[10]) are returns of the joint property and are divided among four old sisters (two sisters in Kabukiran and two other sisters in Barrio Santa Barbara), but other members of the family, who are entitled to shares of the returns of the joint property, do not receive them. Asked for the reason why they do not claim the shares, they said, "We are young people and can work, but they are old." One nephew, an elder brother of M. Dizon, who is a municipal treasurer of other municipality in Bulacan, does not claim a share, either. Thus, although *comunidado* is a form of joint ownership of property, the returns may not be shared equally by each joint owner.

Two of the four surviving daughters of Rafael now live together in the village (No. 10). The elder lives on pension of about 150 pesos a month for her late husband who had served in the U.S. Navy. She is said to be the most affluent person in the village, but lives a modest life, weaving *buntal* hats all day together with her sister. How Rafael Corpus acquired this land is not clearly established, but it is said that Rafael, once a tenant farmer, began to buy small parcels of land in the 1910's from landlords in Baliuag, and that he exerted great efforts to turn waste land into paddy fields.

(2) The Gastons: This family lives in the *kalsada* of Baliuag. Their land was accumulated before and after World War II by the Gastons' father who was engaged in rice milling and in selling *uway*, material for *buntal* hats. At one time the area of land totaled 95 hectares. When the father died in 1959, the land, then 45 hectares, was divided into equal

[8]In Tagalog joint ownership by siblings is called *Pagaari ng mga Kapatid*, but the Spanish term *comunidado* is more commonly used.

[9]Figures in the parentheses after personal names refer to the number given to householders in Barrio Kabukiran by this writer for his survey. All names and particulars are listed in appendix A.

[10]Cavan is a common measure of rice and corn in the Philippines, and is equivalent to 75 liters. One cavan of palay is 44 kilograms.

amounts among one daughter and two sons. The land is now managed by the elder son, a high school teacher, because his sister lives in Manila and his younger brother is still a student. A considerable portion of the 45 hectares has been sold in the past few years, and the land still remaining in Kabukiran is 15 hectares. According to them, their income from farm-rent and from the sale of land is spent to pay for living expenses and educational expenses for the younger brother. The elder brother handles matters with tenants, not delegating management to a *katiwala*, but he seems to make little effort to increase farm productivity.

(3) Segundo Cruz: Cruz was born in Malolos and was formerly a retailer of salt. He now lives in the *kalsada*. While he himself is busy making rounds of his land, his wife sells *uway*. He owns 12.5 hectares of land in Kabukiran, of which 11 hectares are paddy fields. He bought this land at the price of 2,000 pesos per hectare in 1953 through an *ahente* from J. Orosa, who inherited the land from Jacinto Ponce. Cruz also owns 18 hectares of land in San Antonio, Nueva Ecija. Being the most active in management of land among all the landowners, he frequently visits his tenants by bicycle during the farming season and gives them instructions about farming. He also leveled his land using a bulldozer and turned single-crop fields into double-crop fields. In this regard he is an uncommon innovator among the landlords in the area. As to Macapagal's Land Reform Code of 1963 (Republic Act No. 3844), he says, "Under this law honest men lose. Even though tenants are converted to leaseholders they do not have sufficient financial resources, so that they cannot last in the position."

(4) Marcial Roldan: In addition to managing a rice mill in Baliuag, Roldan runs a poultry farm and a hardware shop. He also owns a hardware and dry goods store in Manila. His land in the village is 6.5 hectares, of which 6.4 hectares are paddy fields. He obtained this land in 1934, and also owns land in Barrio Matangtubig and Barrio Santo Niño.

(5) Ireneo Rico: Rico is an engineer employed by the Bureau of Public Works. He bought three hectares of land from Gaston in 1963. It is a very common practice for merchants, salaried employees, and public servants to buy land when they have saved some money. Rico is a good example of such a practice.

(6) Pablo Feliciano: Feliciano manages a bakery on Highway. Like Ireneo Rico, he bought one hectare of land from Gaston in 1963.

Next, the landlords who live outside Baliuag will be introduced.

(7) Miguel Salvador: So far as the land owned in the village is con-

cerned, Salvador is the biggest landlord with 26 hectares of land including 20 hectares of paddy field. Formerly he was farming in the suburbs
of Manila, but as urban sprawl proceeded he sold his land and bought
new land in this village for 65,000 pesos in 1956. He now lives in Quezon
City and owns rental housing as well as engaging in commerce. He does
not employ a *katiwala* but personally manages the land using his jeep to
travel between Quezon City and the village. Of 11 tenants, two are
his relatives.

(8) Apolonia Ramoy: Ramoy also lives in Quezon City, and owned
a farm there. But when urbanization spread Ramoy sold it and bought
land in Baliuag from Gaston in 1958. Tenants pay her fixed rent in kind
instead of share rent. Ramoy does not employ a *katiwala*.

(9) Joaquin Gonzales: Gonzales was born in Baliuag but now manu-
factures and sells radio sets in Manila. In the village he owns 9.4 hectares of land, of which 9.2 hectares is paddy fields. Besides this, he is
said to have a considerable area of land in other villages.

(10) Pereglina Tan: The Tans are one of the old *propiyetaryo* in
Baliuag. Now living in Manila, she owns apartments and houses for rent.
In Baliuag she owns 62.8 hectares of land centering in Barrio Pinag-
barilan. Her land in Kabukiran is nine hectares. Her daughter, Salud
Calderon, manages the land, employing as *katiwala* a tenant farmer
named E. Carillo, who lives in Concepcion and farms land in Pinagbarilan.

(11) Mauro Ocampo: Ocampo lives in Meycauayan, Bulacan. In
1960, he bought 18 hectares of land in the village from Rafael Gonzales
and the Gastons and 20 hectares of land in Telapayong, Apalit, from
Emilio Rustia. He employs V. Robles, who was once Rustia's *katiwala,*
as his *namumuisan.* Since he rarely visits his land, even his name is not
known among his tenants. Since the harvest of *dayatan* or secondary crop
in 1964, tenants have been paying Ocampo *buwis* or fixed rent in kind
(see Chap. VII, Sec. 2).

(12) The Roman Catholic Church: Land owned by the Church is generally called *capilla* or *kapilya*, but in this region it is usually called *mitra*.
The Church owns 134.5 hectares of land in Telapayong and Suliban and
21 hectares in Santo Niño and is the biggest landowner in Baliuag. A very
small portion of 134 hectares of *mitra*, that is 2.6 hectares, is located in
Kabukiran. The ownership of *mitra* belongs to the archbishop in Manila.
Although the date when it came into existence is not known, *mitra* is said
to be the accumulation of land contributed to the Church by farmers

during the Spanish regime.[11] The *mitra* in Baliuag is divided into three parts and rented to *arrendadors*[12] for fixed fees. Fifty-two hectares of *mitra* land, including 2.6 hectares in Kabukiran, are rented to the widow of the former Provincial Governor Juan Carlos (villagers call her Viuda de Carlos), for the *buwis* of 6,000 pesos a year. Since the contract between the archbishop and Carlos expired in 1963, a parish priest has been aspiring to the position of *arrendador*. On the other hand, tenants have been demanding to conclude a contract of leasehold directly with the archbishop with no *arrendador* intervening (see Chap. VII, Sec. 2).

Finally, we shall see an example of owner farmer.

(13) Roberto Cuaderno: Cuaderno is a merchant who lives in the *kalsada*. In addition to running a general store, he is a broker of *uway* and *buntal* hats. He buys semi-finished hats in Baliuag, delivers them to subcontractors for final processing and sells finished products to exporters in Manila. He also raises hogs. He owns 1.1 hectares of land in the village, half of which was inherited by his wife when her father, B. Jaime, died. Jaime's land, 2.2 hectares, was divided among his four children, and later Cuaderno bought the share of one inheritor. Until 1956 Cuaderno had rented his land to a tenant, but then the land was resumed and now is farmed by his third son. He also owns six hectares of land in Barrio Matangtubig, which is rented to tenants. Cuaderno is one of three owner farmers cultivating in the village, but his farm is poorly managed.

From the examples cited above, it is obvious that most of the present landowners in the village obtained their land after World War II; actually, only seven of the present 25 landowners owned land before World War II. Large plots of land owned by a small number of *propiyetaryo* have been divided into smaller and smaller plots in the succession of inheritance, and the fragmentation of landownership has been accelerated through the sale of small plots since World War II. Changes in landownership occur partly because some *propiyetaryo* go bankrupt, but mainly because big landlords sell parts of their farmland to invest in real estate and commercial enterprises in Manila. There are no big landlords who have made positive investments in industrial manufacturing, however.

Most of new small landlords are merchants in Baliuag and Manila, and

[11]There are many stories told by villagers about contributions of land to the Church. They claim the land was taken away against the wills of their forefathers.

[12]He is also called by the name of *hacendero* in the region.

they buy land with money they have saved. Such landownership is not so much investment in land as a form of property management that brings social prestige to owners, and is characterized by a strong touch of parasitism. As we have seen earlier, the landlord who strives to increase land productivity through additional investment in land is the exception. On the other hand, in addition to Cuaderno, there are two small landowners who themselves farm. They own and farm land in the village but live in Kalantipay.

Fluidity in landownership is relatively high. In many cases *ahente* finds prospective buyers of land. Land prices have been increasing, and the price of double-crop paddy fields, which was 4,000 to 5,000 pesos per hectare in 1958-59, is 6,000 to 7,000 pesos in 1964. Such a rise in land price is attributed not to an increase in land productivity but to non-agricultural factors.

CHAPTER V

Cultivators and Crops

1. Farming Households

In Barrio Kabukiran there are 36 farming households which have more or less stable tenure of their land. Two of the remaining eight households farm small portions of other tenant farmers' land seasonally, but since their tenure is not stable, they are counted as non-farming households. Of the 36 farming households, five households farm 9.5 hectares of land outside the village, and one of them has no tenure of land in the village. Such a practice to cultivate a distant farmland is usually called *dayudayu-han*. All the farming households in the village are tenant farmers. Antonio Corpus (No. 2) and Manuel Dizon (No. 15) have claim to one-twelfth and one-sixth, respectively, of their joint property, but since their right is more latent than manifest, as mentioned above, they should be considered tenant farmers.

The land cultivated by each farming household ranges from one to five hectares (Table 12); households which cultivate one to three hectares of land number 26 (73 per cent of all the households), and the average

Table 12. Farming Households in Kabukiran by
Area of Cultivated Land (1964)

Area of cultivated land	Number of farming households	Number of farming households living in the village	Number of farming households living outside the village
0.5 ∼ 0.9 ha.	6	—	6
1.0 ∼ 1.9	25	14	11
2.0 ∼ 2.9	24	12	12
3.0 ∼ 3.9	5	3	2
4.0 ∼ 4.9	2	2	—
5.0 ∼ 5.9	5	5	—
6.0 and more	—	—	—
Total	67	36	31

Source: Field survey by the author.

amount of cultivated land is 2.5 hectares. Since the average of land cultivated by palay farms in Baliuag is 2.2 hectares, and that in the Province
of Bulacan is 1.9 hectares, the figure for Kabukiran is relatively high.
The distribution of households in the village by the area of cultivated
land, however, shows a pattern not different from that in the municipality
or in the province in general (Table 13). Needless to say, the area of

Table 13. Comparison of Farming Households by
Area of Cultivated Land (1960, 1964)

Area of cultivated land	Province of Bulacan (1960)	Municipality of Baliuag (1960)	Barrio Kabukiran (1964)
under 0.5 ha.	1,254 (3.9%)	23 (1.5%)	— (—)
0.5 ~ 0.9	1,463 (4.6)	15 (1.0)	6 (9.0%)
1.0 ~ 1.9	12,753 (40.2)	583 (37.9)	25 (37.3)
2.0 ~ 2.9	9,349 (29.3)	563 (36.6)	24 (35.8)
3.0 ~ 3.9	3,700 (11.6)	211 (13.7)	5 (7.5)
4.0 ~ 4.9	1,402 (4.4)	67 (4.4)	2 (3.0)
5.0 ~ 9.9	1,556 (4.9)	49 (3.2)	5 (7.5)
10.0 ~ 19.9	325 (1.0)	25 (1.6)	— (—)
20.0 ~ 49.9	35 (0.1)	— (—)	— (—)
50.0 ~ 99.9	8 (0)	1 (0)	— (—)
100.0 and more	9 (0)	— (—)	— (—)
Total	31,854 (100%)	1,537 (100%)	67 (100%)

Remarks: Figures for the Province of Bulacan and Municipality of Baliuag
are based on 1960 census. Those for Barrio kabukiran are as of
April, 1964.

cultivated land alone does not give a complete picture of the stratification
of farming households. Since monoculture of palay prevails in the village,
the productivity of farmland is dependent on whether paddy fields yield
one or two crops a year. Table 14 gives the breakdown of households
by the area of cultivated land multiplied by the number of crops per year.
In this breakdown the largest cultivated land is 10.0 hectares, and 26
households cluster in the two to six hectare range, with the average size
being 3.8 hectares.

Almost all the farming households are engaged in side jobs of one kind
or another. Disregarding *buntal* hat weaving by housewives, only two
farming households, which are in the seven to eight hectare range, are
engaged in full-time farming, and the remaining 34 farming households
are considerably dependent on side jobs (Table 15). Of the latter, 26 are

Table 14.   Farming Households in Kabukiran by Gross
Area Cultivated (1964)

Gross area cultivated	Number of farming households	Number of farming households living in the village	Number of farming households living outside the village
0.5~ 0.9 ha.	1	—	1
1.0~ 1.9	16	4	12
2.0~ 2.9	14	9	5
3.0~ 3.9	9	5	4
4.0~ 4.9	9	5	4
5.0~ 5.9	11	7	4
6.0~ 6.9	3	2	1
7.0~ 7.9	1	1	—
8.0~ 8.9	1	1	—
9.0~ 9.9	1	1	—
10.0~10.9	1	1	—
Total	67	36	31

Remarks: Gross area cultivated is the total area of *panag-araw* and
dayatan in a year.
Source: Field survey by the author.

Table 15.   Side Jobs of Farming Households Living in Kabukiran (1964)

Gross area cultivated	Households engaged in full-time farming	Households engaged in side jobs						Total
		More in farming than in side jobs			Engaged primarily in side jobs			
		Self-employed	Self-employed and engaged in wage labor	Engaged in wage labor	Self-employed and engaged in wage labor	Engaged in wage labor		
1.0~ 2.9 ha.	—	—	—	6	4	3		13
3.0~ 4.9	—	—	—	9	—	1		10
5.0~ 6.9	—	2	2	5	—	—		9
7.0~10.0	2	—	2	—	—	—		4
Total	2	2	4	20	4	4		36

Source: Field survey by the author.

engaged more in farming than in side jobs. Six of this group are self-employed (four *karitela* drivers, one pedicab driver, one *cantina*[1] keeper). It is worth noting that these six are among households which hold five hectares and more. As for the remaining 20 households, heads or members of households work for wages as farm wage labor.

On the other hand, the number of households which are more dependent on side jobs than on farming is eight, and except for the one working in the municipal office, they are engaged in farm labor, and cultivate less than three hectares of land. Even in this group of the lowest stratum, some are self-employed such as one *sarisari* store keeper, one barber, two pedicab drivers and one *karitela* driver.

As mentioned before, the farming households which farm land in the village but do not live in the village number 31, and they farm 52.5 hectares or 39 per cent of cultivated land in the village. The breakdown of these households by the place of their residence is as follows: adjacent barrios, 14; the *kalsada,* 13; and other municipalities, four (Map 7). Those from adjacent barrios are further broken down into: Kalantipay, two; Suliban, six; Pinagbarilan, three; Telapayong, two; and Pagala, one. They live 0.5 to three kilometers away from their farms, and have been farming the land for many years. Many from the *kalsada* live in Santo Cristo and Concepcion, barrios on the northwest of the *kalsada.* Since they must cover the distance of four to six kilometers to come, it takes more than one hour if they are coming with *kalabaw* and some 20 minutes even by bicycle. Of 13 such households, seven had lived in the village before World War II and the rest have started farming in recent years. The four households from other municipalities consist of three which live in San Luis and San Simon, in the Province of Pampanga, (four to five kilometers away from the village), and one who was born in the village and who now lives in Malolos and comes to stay at his relative's house in the village in the farming season.

The size of the plots in the village cultivated by farming households living outside ranges from 0.5 to three hectares (Table 14), and the average size is 1.7 hectares, much smaller than that of the farming households living in the village. The actual size of holdings of farming households living outside could not be obtained but it was estimated that more than 80 per cent of those households cultivate land only in Kabukiran.

We can say that the cultivators, living outside but cultivating land in

---

[1]This *cantina,* a small store, sells drinks and candies to school children.

Map 7.   Cultivators from Other Barrios (1964)

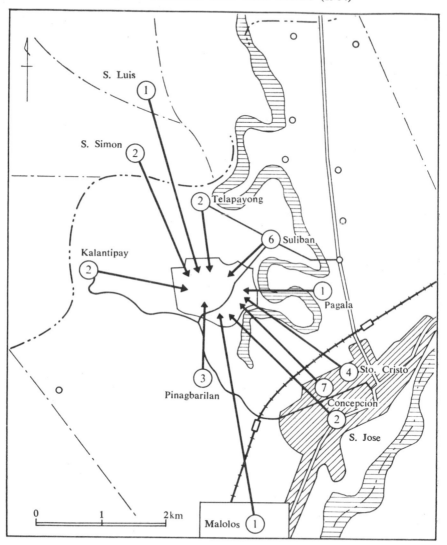

Kabukiran, are living relatively close to the land they work, compared with such cultivators in the Municipality of Baliuag in general. But they come to attend to their farms only once or twice a week except in the farming season, and their farm operation leaves much to be desired. Out of 31 such cultivators, only four have farm huts called *kubo* in the village. In most cases, the yield of crops harvested by those cultivators, is smaller than that of cultivators living on the farm. Many of those cultivators, especially those who live in the *kalsada,* are engaged more in side jobs than in farming. One of them is a bus driver who engages in farmwork only in the busy farming season.

2. Means of Production

Land

As land use, landownership, and the scale of farm management have already been touched on, here other factors concerning land will be mentioned.

Map 8 shows plots of farmland cultivated by respective households. Plots are usually located around farmhouses. Twenty-eight farming households have their paddy fields in one place, and eight have their paddy fields in two places. There is none which has its paddy field in three or more places. Plots of paddy fields are divided into smaller parcels by *pilapil* (levees or dikes); usually one hectare of land is divided into five to eight parcels. Since there is no feeder road, farmers walk on *pilapil* carrying farm implements on their shoulders, and *kalabaw* (water buffalo) tread on plants.

An explanation of the unit of measure for land is in order here. In the Philippines the official unit of land area is hectare, but in this region the amount of seed to be sown in paddy fields is commonly used to indicate the area, e.g., "paddy fields of one cavan." Since one hectare of paddy fields needs 20 gantas of palay, or unhulled rice, (25 gantas make one cavan), "paddy fields of one cavan" would equal 1.25 hectares. Payments for such labor as transplanting or reaping are usually made on the basis of area in cavan. In this monograph, however, area in hectare, not area in cavan, will be used to avoid confusion, unless the use of the latter is more appropriate.

Capital investment in land is extremely small. At most concrete pipes are laid under *pilapil* to guide water from watercourses into paddy fields. The only landlord who attempted land improvement is S. Cruz mentioned above. In 1961 Cruz leveled down six hectares of land, using a bulldozer, so that single-crop fields were turned into double-crop fields. This resulted in an increase of productivity and it is said that the land, which yielded 19 cavans of palay, now produces 40 to 50 cavans in the regular crop and 30 cavans in the secondary crop.

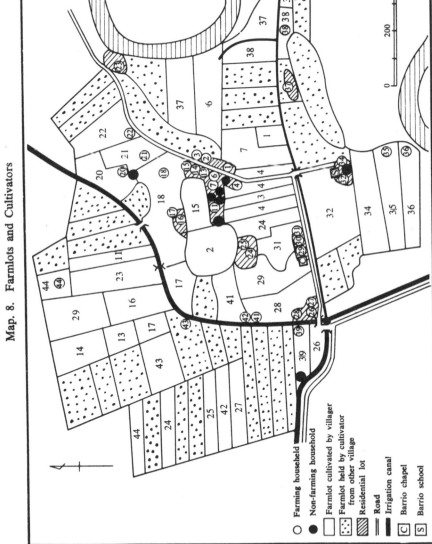

Map. 8. Farmlots and Cultivators

○ Farming household
● Non-farming household
▢ Farmlot cultivated by villager
▦ Farmlot held by cultivator from other village
▨ Residential lot
▬ Road
▮ Irrigation canal
C Barrio chapel
S Barrio school

As for residential land, 19 households live in permanent residential land. Only the descendants of Rafael Corpus own residential land. Other families who rent farmland have built their houses on land received without payment from the landlords. The remaining 17 families have built their houses on parts of paddy fields.

Irrigation

Water supply facilities are one of the most important means of production in the village. Since the village is covered by the ARIS, the large scale national irrigation project, it is favored by far better conditions than is the average Philippine village. The irrigation pump which plays an important role in other regions is owned solely by one landlord, M. Salvador, but it is rarely utilized.

First, let us have a look at the ARIS project. The project was to acquire irrigation water from the Angat River by construction of a dam, three meters high and 524 meters in length, at Bustos. The water was to be supplied to farmland in the southern part of the Central Luzon Plain through canals on both sides of the river. Construction work was started in 1922, and water was first delivered in 1926. The irrigation system benefits 26,980 hectares of paddy fields in 13 municipalities (nine in the Province of Bulacan and four in the Province of Pampanga) and its network of watercourses, including both main canals and laterals, totals 550 kilometers in length (Map 9). It was by far the largest irrigation project undertaken during the American rule, and even today it is the largest among the 63 irrigation systems under direct administration of the Bureau of Public Works.[2]

Laterals branch away from the main canals, and sub-laterals, usually called *kanal,* branch away from the laterals. At all points of ramification there are water gates which are under the direct management of the ARIS office. Terminal watercourses called *sanga* are built by the farmers themselves. At the *salahan,* or point where *sanga* branch away from lateral, simple concrete poles are struck into the ground, and wooden boards are used to regulate the flow of water. That is, when water is needed, the *salahan* is closed so that the water level will be raised and water will flow

[2]Other large-scale irrigation systems are that of the Agno River in the Province of Pangasinan (25,000 hectares), and that of the Magat River in the Province of Isabela (23,000 hectares). There are five systems covering 10,000 hectares, seven systems covering 5,000 to 10,000 hectares, 31 systems covering 1,000 to 5,000 hectares. See "Management and Operation of Irrigation and Drainage Systems."

Map 9. The Angat River Irrigation System

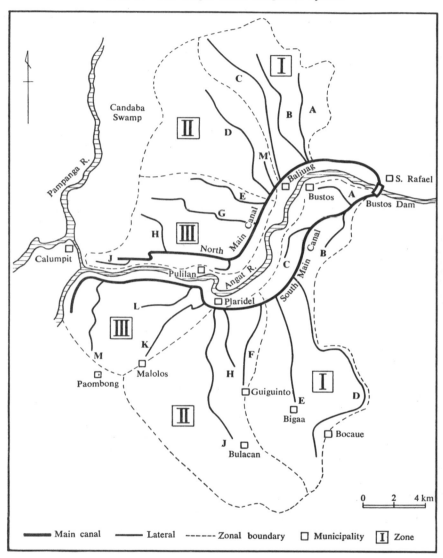

Main canal —— Lateral —----- Zonal boundary □ Municipality Ⅰ Zone

into *sanga*. When water is not needed, intake of *sanga* is stuffed with mud and straw.

The process through which ARIS water is supplied for paddy fields is very complicated. Since the amount of water is not sufficient, paddy fields on the north side of the river and those on the south side of the river have water supplied in alternate years during the dry season. For example, paddy fields on the north side of the river begin to get water from the Main Canal on March 28 in odd-numbered years. In such years preparations for the secondary crop, called *dayatan,* can be started very early, and most of paddy fields become double-crop land. On the other hand, in even-numbered years water is supplied primarily to paddy fields on the south side of the river during the dry season, so that paddy fields on the north side get water only when there is superfluous supply. Since a full-scale supply of water for the north side begins on June 20, preparations for the *dayatan* are delayed and it becomes impossible for unfavorably located paddy fields to produce the secondary crop.

It must be noted that even in the watering period paddy fields do not get uniform and constant supplies of water. On both sides of the river paddy fields are divided into three zones, and each zone has alternate full-supply, partial-supply, and no-supply periods, with each period lasting for one week. Since Barrio Kabukiran belongs to Zone II on the north side, the supply of water for the village was officially begun on June 20 in 1964, but the first week, June 20-26, was a no-supply week, followed by a partial-supply week, June 27-July 3, by a full-supply week, July 4-10, then by another no-supply week, July 11-17, thus the cycle being repeated.

The ARIS district is divided into 13 divisions. The supervisor of each division, called watermaster, supervises six ditchtenders and one gatekeeper. The watermaster is responsible for the opening and closing of water gates and for the maintenance of watercourses. Fees for the use of irrigation water are 12 pesos per hectare whether paddy fields are single- or double-crop fields.[3] The watermaster collects the fees from landowners.

As outlined above, it is obvious that this area is among those in the Philippines favored so far as an irrigation system is concerned. Yet many problems remain to be solved. First and foremost, there is a shortage of water. Even in ordinary years the water shortage makes it impossible for

---

[3]In April 1967 irrigation fee rates were revised. In the case of paddy fields, the new rates were 25 pesos per hectare for the first crop, 35 pesos per hectare for the second crop, and 35 pesos and 50 centavos per hectare for double-crops. This amount of fee for double-crops is equal to the sum of the fee for the first crop and 30 per cent of the fee for the second crop. "Ang Bagong Halaga ng Bayad sa Patubig ay di Nakabibigat sa mga Magsasaka" (Sta. Cruz River Irrigation System Office, n.d.) p. 2.

the fringes of the ARIS district to have two crops a year, and other areas also suffer from the water shortage in June, the transplanting season, and in the August-October period. The writer often heard cultivators in Kabukiran saying that abundant water supplies would increase crops, as well as make possible the harvesting of two crops a year. The water shortage is not the only problem, however. There is the problem of maintaining watercourses as well. Leakage or wasting of water due to poor maintenance of watercourses is said to be considerable. Since the shortage of ditchtenders requires one ditchtender to take care of the laterals for 300 to 400 hectares of paddy fields, maintenance is not adequate, resulting in inefficient distribution of water.

The biggest problem seems to be the lack of voluntary organizations to facilitate efficient water use among the cultivators themselves. For example, the maintenance of watercourses is left entirely to the ARIS authorities, as few farmers volunteer to cut the water-grasses which obstruct the flow of water. No attempt appears to have been made to organize cooperative work for the maintenance of watercourses. What is worse, as was often observed, cultivators raise the water level at *salahan* in order to take water into their own paddy fields without regard to the condition of plants in other cultivators' fields. They also remove partition boards at *salahan* as they please if they think water flow is too much. There is no mutual regulation of the use of water among farmers. In other words, a sort of anarchy prevails concerning the use of water at the village level.[4] To cope with this situation, the ARIS office recently began to organize an irrigators' association for each lateral area. The purposes of these associations was to enlist the cooperation of the cultivators for the maintenance of watercourses and to mediate disputes over water use among cultivators. However, in 1964, real progress has not yet been made in this direction.

Farm Equipment

Utilization of farm tractors and large threshing machines called *telyadora* is widely spread, but there are no such machines in the village. The only machine in the village is a rarely used pump owned by Miguel Salvador.

Farming implements owned by the average cultivator are wooden plows with iron blades (*araro*) and harrows (*suyod*). Many farming households

[4]What this fact means in the village society will be discussed in Chapter XII.

do not own carts or sledges to be used on muddy roads. Three rotary weeders manipulated by hand are said to exist in the village. For reaping palay, small serrated sickle called *lilik* are used, since *yatab*,[5] common in other regions, are not used in the area. In *panag-araw* (regular crop) harvesting *telyadora* is hired for threshing, and in *dayatan* cultivators thresh the palay by striking the rice stalks against bamboo platforms or by treading on it. Hulling machines are not needed because the rice is stored and sold unhulled except for domestic consumption. *Karitela* is used for transporting palay.

Livestock and Grass

In the Philippines it is a common practice for tenant farmers to own domestic animals. Of the 36 farming households in Kabukiran, two households own three *kalabaw* (water buffalo), four households own two, 26 households borrow one each from their landlords. All told, there are 42 *kalabaw* in the village (Table 16). The price of one *kalabaw* is about 600 to 700 pesos. The two farmers who borrow *kalabaw* from landlords are relatives of the landlords. One of the two farmers who do not own a *kalabaw* is Lucas Adeva (No. 30), who rents and farms land outside the village and borrows a *kalabaw* occasionally from his landlord; the other is Domingo Villanueva (No. 7) who borrows his father's *kalabaw* free of charge when it is not being used, and who also depends more heavily on farm tractors than do the other cultivators.

Other than *kalabaw,* large domestic animals in the village include a total of seven cows kept by four households. Except for one cow owned by Antonio Corpus (No. 2), these cows are owned by landlords and loaned to cultivators. Rodolfo Sanchez (No. 29) milks his own *kalabaw* and a borrowed cow and delivers six bottles[6] of fresh milk to the *kalsada* every morning for 30 centavos per bottle.

In addition, there are a total of six horses for *karitela* owned by five households. Hogs, chickens, and ducks also are raised for domestic consumption.

Villagers are free to mow grass to be used as feed for domestic animals or as green manure, whether it grows on *pilapil* or on grass land. Paddy fields are also open to public use after the palay has been harvested. In other words, no ownership is claimed over grass and the stumps of palay.

[5]*Yatab* is a knife fastened across a wooden handle and used exclusively for harvesting of palay. Palay is reaped panicle by panicle.

[6]This bottle appears to be approximately half a pint in capacity.

Table 16. The Number of *Kalabaw* (1964)

Number of *kalabaw* kept by each household	Number of households	Number of *kalabaw*
3	2	6
2	4	8
1	26	26
0	2	—
kalabaw borrowed	2	2
Total	36	42

Source: Field survey by the author.

At the time when palay is growing, however, pasturing domestic animals is not permitted, and the animals must be kept on leash or within pens. It is said that the large amount of labor needed to feed keeps the number of *kalabaw* small.

3.   Patterns of Cultivation

Introduction of Double-Cropping

Since climate and the cropping pattern are varied in the Philippines, many inter-regional differences exist in the crop calendar. Within Central Luzon, the pattern of the rice-growing is not uniform, but is determined by a number of factors, such as whether paddy fields are single- or double-crop land, whether irrigation water can be easily obtained or not, and when paddy fields began to get irrigation water (Fig. 4).

In the case of single-crop fields, cultivators begin plowing the fields and preparing the seedbeds after the rainy season sets in. They sow seeds in the latter half of July and transplant seedlings into paddy fields between late August and mid-September. The popular variety of rice is *intan* of the non-seasonal variety whose growing period is about 145 days; *intan* is harvested between late December and mid-January, 110 to 120 days after transplanting. *Wagwag* is most delicious and is therefore sold for the highest price, but since it is one of the seasonal varieties,[7] the time

[7]Since most of the palay indigenous to the Philippines are of the seasonal variety, they bloom out irrespective of the time of transplanting and their harvesting time is determined. Therefore, they cannot be grown for secondary crops. See College of Agriculture, University of the Philippines, *Rice Production in the Philippines* (College, Laguna, n.d.), p. 15. In addition to *wagwag, burma* and *serup* are popular seasonal varieties in this area.

Fig. 4. Crop Calendar

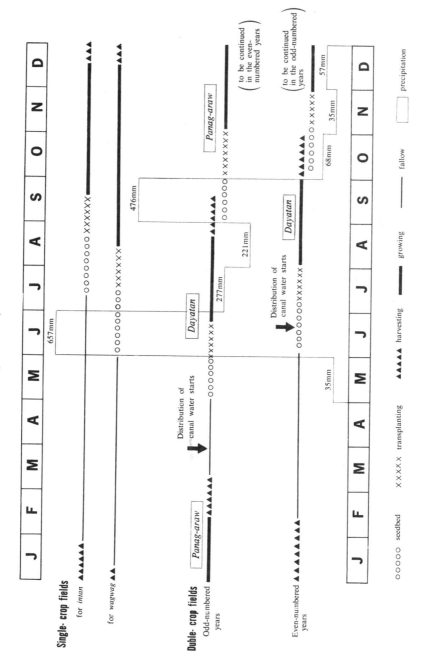

of harvest for *wagwag* is definite and its period for maturity is about 180 days. *Wagwag* is normally transplanted between July and early August, and harvested in late December. Thus, the basic cropping pattern consists of transplanting between July and September and harvesting in December for the regular crop, called *panag-araw,* in this region.[8]

When irrigation water is easily available and cultivation of a secondary crop is possible, the *panag-araw* is delayed and the secondary crop is grown first; in terms of time, the secondary crop precedes the regular crop. For *dayatan,* the secondary crop,[9] the early maturing varieties such as *binato* and *horai* are chosen (maturity times are about 120 days); for *panag-araw,* the non-seasonal variety such as *intan* is chosen because its planting time is delayed.

In odd-numbered years when ARIS water is available early in the season, seed for the *dayatan* is sown in the first half of May, transplanting takes place 30 days later, between late May and mid-June, and palay is harvested 90 days later, between late August and mid-September. During the month after the *dayatan* is harvested, preparation of fields and seedlings for the *panag-araw* is made, transplanting takes place between early and late October, and the *panag-araw* is harvested four months later, between early January and early February. In even-numbered years, the whole cycle is delayed by one to one and a half months; the *dayatan* transplanting takes place between early and late July and the crop is harvested between early and late October, while the *panag-araw* transplanting takes place between early and late November, and the crop is harvested between late February and early March.

It is rather recently that such a double-cropping pattern has been established. Although irrigation facilities were developed early, single-cropping had been the rule for many years, and three crops per two years had been possible only where water was easily available. In Kabukiran, too, single-cropping had been a common practice. Since 1947, however, *dayatan* has been attempted in low paddy fields on the north side of Lateral-D. It was as recently as 1960-1962 that *dayatan* crop as is practiced today

---

[8]According to the definition of terms in the Census of the Philippines, the dry season crop, commonly called *palagad* or *panag-araw,* which is usually planted in paddy fields with irrigation, is classified as "second crop lowland palay." (*Census of the Philippines 1960: Agriculture,* Vol. II, p. xiii). However, since *panag-araw* occupies a principal position in the whole agricultural pattern in this region, it is regarded as the regular crop.

[9]Since in other regions of the Philippines secondary crops are grown in the dry season after regular crops have been harvested, they are commonly called *palagad,* or dry-season crops.

came to be widely spread. The major reason for the popularization of *dayatan* has been the diffusion of early maturing varieties such as *binato* and *horai* mentioned above and of *intan* which is a non-seasonal variety and whose yield is very stable. These new varieties of palay have made possible delaying *panag-araw* crop and introducing *dayatan*. Other reasons have been the improvement of the dam and watercourses, and the diffusion of fertilizers.

The recent trend of the increase of double-cropping of palay in this region is shown in Table 17. In 1939 the second crop was found only in the municipalities located in the lower part of the Province of Bulacan, such as Hagonoy, Calumpit, Paombong and Plaridel. In the Municipality of Baliuag the second crop was not observed in 1939, but in 1948 it occupied more than seven hundred hectares of land. By 1960 the area increased to four times the 1948 area, and now the second crop has a considerably high position in regard to planted area and production.

Table 17.   Increase of Double-Cropping of Palay (1939–60)

	1939		1948		1960	
	Area planted (ha.)	Production (cavans)	Area planted (ha.)	Production (cavans)	Area planted (ha.)	Production (cavans)
Province of Bulacan						
Total	66,528	2,192,715	53,066	1,737,744	67,730	2,308,007
First crop lowland	60,979	2,036,785	41,567	1,377,789	53,819	1,864,579
Second crop lowland*	3,064	100,717	10,185	329,668	10,196	354,999
Upland & Kaingin**	2,485	55,413	58	1,049	3,715	88,429
Municipality of Baliuag						
Total	3,727	196,698	2,435	119,920	6,445	245,270
First corp lowland	3,678	196,002	1,642	82,253	3,537	147,011
Second crop lowland*	—	—	735	36,618	2,902	98,199
Upland & Kaingin**	49	696	58	1,049	6	60

* See note 8 of this chapter.
**See Appendix B.
Source: Census of the Philippines, 1939, 1948, 1960.

Farming Practices

First, let us look at double-crop land. Paddy fields are plowed lightly with the use of *kalabaw* or farm tractors in the dry season (March-April).

Called *isinasalan* (light touching), this plowing is aimed at removing the roots of weeds. When the rainy season sets in, seedbeds are prepared. In even-numbered years when the supply of ARIS water is delayed, cultivators sometimes cannot use their own paddy fields as seedbeds. In such a case they ask their relatives or friends for the use of part of the latter's paddy fields where it is possible to raise seedlings without irrigation. Usually it is not necessary to inform the owner of the land of such use of paddy fields, nor to pay any fee. Seeds used are part of the preceding year's crop. "Certified seeds" are not popular at all. Rarely is a selection of seeds conducted. Half a cavan of seeds is sown in an oblong plot called *kama,* which means a bed. Since much harm is inflicted on seeds by birds, many cultivators do not want to sow seeds earlier than others. At the time of sowing seeds scarecrows called *tautauhan* are set up. After rain has softened the paddy fields the cultivators till them repeatedly with *kalabaw*-drawn plows (*araro*) and harrows (*suyod*).[10] Immediately before transplanting, the cultivators level paddy fields most thoroughly. Plowing and harrowing of paddy fields are often performed on a mutual assistance basis called *palusong.*

Before transplanting the seedlings are pulled and bundled with bamboo strings. This work is called *bunot* and the cultivators rarely do it by themselves. For this work they hire *namumunot* (seedling-pullers) and pay them in accordance with the number of bundles they pull. The transplanting itself is completely dependent on hired labor. Planting workers called *manananim* organize themselves into groups of 20 to 30 members led by foremen called *kabisilya* or *punong-sugo,* and *manananim*'s groups contract for the transplanting. The common method of planting is a traditional irregular one called *ordinario.* In 1964 the *masagana* method of straight row planting, which once had been adopted by several cultivators, was not observed in Kabukiran. Since cost for *masagana* planting is more expensive than that for *ordinario,* the former has been on the decline.[11]

Very little effort is made to weed paddy fields, although some effort was made in the case of *masagana.* Many cultivators do not apply fertilizers for *dayatan.* Like transplanting, the harvesting which takes place between mid-September and late October is dependent on hired labor. Since the ground is wet and soft at this time, machines cannot be brought

---

[10]In many cases tractors are hired and the ground is broken up with arrow-wheels.

[11]In December 1965, it was observed that the *masagana* system again was adopted by several cultivators in this village at the planting of *panag-araw.*

into the paddy fields. Therefore reapers called *manggagapas* carry bundles of palay on their heads to dry ground such as *bakuran,* residential lots, and roadsides where they thresh the palay by striking it against *hampasan* or bamboo platforms, or by treading on it.

The growing of the *panag-araw* is about the same as that of the *dayatan.* In harvesting the *panag-araw,* however, dried palay is made into bundles, which in turn are piled up into *sipok* or stacks, one to 1.5 meter high in the paddy fields which have dried up by that time. When the *sipok* are further dried, they are made into still bigger cylindrical stacks (*mandala*) three to four meters high. For threshing palay, large threshing machines (*telyadora*) pulled by tractors are commonly used. For fertilizing paddy fields, complete fertilizers and sulphuric ammonium are applied twice, but the amounts are small, and the amount of manure applied is also small.

It is difficult to obtain correct figures for the yield. It differs considerably from year to year and farm by farm. R. Cuaderno who lives in *kalsada* and tills one hectare of land, for example, harvested 55 cavans for *dayatan* in 1963, but only four cavans for *panag-araw* in March 1964, because of damage by wild rats. Cuaderno's case may be exceptional, and yet it is not unusual for many farming households to experience quite different yields from year to year. Through interviews with cultivators, this writer found the yield per hectare ranges from 21 to 80 cavans. But it seems safe to estimate that the standard yield of the *dayatan* crop using *binato* variety is 35 to 40 cavans, and that of the *panag-araw* crop using *intan* is 50 to 55 cavans.[12] Actual yield, however, falls short of the standard due to natural disasters and other damage.

In a small area (6.5 hectares) of marshy field called *bana* in the center and southern edge of the village, seeds are directly broadcast into paddy fields, and 2-4-D is used for weeding. Yields are low and unstable because of weeds, however.

The technical level of the farming methods in the village may be regarded as average by the standard of the Municipality of Baliuag. An agricultural extension worker from the Agricultural Productivity Commission (formerly the Bureau of Agricultural Extension) was stationed in the village from September 1963 to February 1964; but he was forced to

---

[12]The average yield in irrigated paddy fields in the ARIS district is as follows: *wagwag,* 47 cavans; *intan,* 50 cavans; *binato,* 39 cavans; *horai,* 42 cavans; and *burma,* 50 cavans. ("Irrigation and Drainage") According to an agricultural officer, the highest record of yield in the Municipality of Baliuag was 143 cavans of *intan* per hectare in Barrio Sabang.

leave the village after only six-months because of lack of a sufficient budget allocation.[13]

[13]The Agricultural Productivity Commission designated Baliuag as a pilot municipality for the crop production program and a Production Force was assigned here. Thus in September 1963, 32 agricultural extension workers and 15 female home demonstrators and rural club officers were stationed in almost each barrio of Baliuag. Later, however, many members of the staff were transferred to the Municipality of Plaridel which was proclaimed as the Land Reform District, and a cut in the budget further reduced the permanent staff in Baliuag to only three in April 1964.

A tenant farmer cultivating two hectares of paddy field is hired for wage work as a *namumunot* to prepare seedlings for transplanting. (July 1964)

Town plaza is the center of activities in the municipality. *Karitela* and pedicabs come swarming to plaza. (February 1964)

Town plaza and market viewed from bell tower of the church. (August 1964)

The municipal market of Baliuag. (June 1964)

Bustos Dam and intake of the North Main Canal of the Angat River Irrigation System. (August 1958)

The North Main Canal of the Angat River Irrigation System in the rainy season. Water gate for the Lateral-D is seen at left. (June 1964)

A vehicular road runs through the village. The *bisita* is seen at right. (July 1964)

Slight relief of the land surface causes difference in land use. The lower part is double-crop land, while the elevated land is utilized for single-cropping. (December 1965)

At the beginning of the rainy season farmland is plowed by *palusong* or labor exchange. (July 1964)

Harrowing is also practiced by *palusong*. (July 1964)

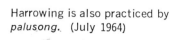

A team of hired laborers, *manananim*, is transplanting palay. Two sons of the cultivator of this farm are working on the team, and receive wage as the others. (July 1964)

The cultivator of this farm (left) is busy carrying seedlings. (July 1964)

A *kabisilya* (left) from neighboring barrio is supervising the work of his team of *manananim*. (July 1964)

Villagers with *lilik* cross the Lateral-D to work as *manggagapas* (reaper) Mt. Arayat is shown at the back. (February 1964)

Manggagapas and *namumulot* rest at a *sipok* stack site. (February 1964)

A team of *manggagapas* led by Mang Ambo is reaping the *panag-araw* crop. (February 1964)

Reaped palay is stacked into a *mandala* for drying. (February 1964)

A *telyadora*, large-size threshing machine, is used for the *panag-araw* harvest. (January 1964)

A *cono*-type rice mill in Bulacan Province. (February 1964)

As soon as the *manggagapas* workers have reaped the palay, a group of *namumulot* starts gleaning and carrying away what they can find. (February 1964)

Children are also able to glean a considerable amount of palay in a short time. (February 1964)

The common cottage industry is *buntal* hat weaving. Most women in the village are engaged in this work. (June 1964)

On market days housewives bring their work to the plaza where they sell the semi-finished hats to, and buy the materials from, dealers waiting at roadside. (June 1964)

The *karitela* is a popular means of transportation in rural barrios, and is an important side business for the villagers. (March 1964)

A stilted nipa house (see Fig. 1) belonging to a tenant farmer with two hectares of land. (July 1964)

The Barrio School of Kabukiran.
(March 1964)

School children on their way home. (March 1964)

An old-fashioned residence of a *propiyetaryo* in poblacion. (June 1964)

A *propiyetaryo* owning some 30 hectares of land has visited his land by bicycle to supervise the harvest. (February 1964)

Masagana method of planting palay. (December 1965)

The Barrio Captain of Kabu-kiran harrowing his tenanted farm. (August 1964)

Back from harvesting work, villagers spend their time in talking and singing in front of *sarisari* store. (February 1964)

The Barrio *bisita* on the day of fiesta.   (April 1964)

Election for officers of Barrio Council of a neighboring barrio. The
seated are the election tellers. (January 1964)

Batalis work is offered by neighbors when a typhoon damaged houses. (July 1964)

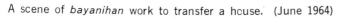

A scene of *bayanihan* work to transfer a house. (June 1964)

CHAPTER VI

Farm Labor

Family Labor

Needless to say, heads of farming households are the basic figures in farm operation. In Barrio Kabukiran, however, such principal works as pulling and bundling of seedlings, transplanting, reaping and threshing are entirely dependent on hired labor, and the ratio of family labor to total labor is very small. The division of work between family and hired labor is truly distinct; when householders and their family members are engaged in the work mentioned above, they pay themselves the same wages that they pay hired laborers. Family labor is employed mainly in plowing and harrowing paddy fields, nursing seedlings, fertilizing, irrigating and controlling paddy fields after transplanting, and raising livestock. Except for plowing and harrowing paddy fields and nursing seedlings, the work required of family labor is not hard. In most cases, heads of households are the only family labor engaged in farming their holdings; only in five of the 36 households do family members join the heads of households in farming. As mentioned in Chapter III, Section 2, the heads of nine farming households are engaged more in side jobs than in farming; among them in Manuel Dizon (No. 15) who works in the municipal hall in daytime although he is responsible for farm operation.

Out of the 62 employed men in the farming households in the village, only 32 are engaged primarily in farming of their own holdings, and the rest are engaged in agricultural and non-agricultural wage work and in services (Table 18). In principle, women are not engaged in farm work on their own holdings. At the time of transplanting, most *manananim* are women, employed as wage workers.

For plowing and harrowing paddy fields, the cultivators perform cooperative work on a basis of labor exchange. This cooperation is called *palusong* or *batalis*. When cultivators go to a neighboring farm on *palusong,* they take with them *kalabaw* and farm implements. Sometimes, more than 10 cultivators get together for *palusong.* The organization of *palusong* is based not so much on kinship, as on local propinquity. *Palusong* is also very fluid in character, as the membership which constitutes

Table 18. Occupations of Population of Farming
Households in Kabukiran (1964)

	Men	Women	Total
Farming	32	—	32
Farm labor	13	17	30
Commerce	—	2	2
Transportation, Services	11	—	11
Non-agricultural wage labor	5	4	9
Public servant	1	—	1
Cottage industry	—	5	5
Sub-total	62	28	90
Unemployed	49	63	112
Total	111	91	202

Source: Field survey by the author.

palusong groups is not fixed but changing.

Hired Labor

Since such work as transplanting, harvesting, threshing, and pulling and bundling of seedlings, is entirely dependent on hired labor instead of family labor, as mentioned above, demands for hired labor are large. This hired labor is supplied jointly from within the village, from outside the village, and from outside the Municipality of Baliuag.

Most non-agricultural households in the village make a living by meeting the demands for hired farm workers. Except for two households of the aged, Josefina Corpus (No. 9) and Lope Corpus (No. 10), six of the eight non-farming households provide 15 farm laborers.[1] What is more important, out of the 36 farming households, there are only three households whose heads or members are not engaged in farm wage work. These three include one household which belongs to the topmost group in the village (Antonio Corpus [No. 2]), one household whose head is engaged in self-employed work as well as in farming (Paulino Araneta [No. 16]), and one household whose head is a public servant (Manuel Dizon [No. 15]). The remaining 33 households provide a total of 71 farm laborers (50 men, including 24 heads of households, and 21 women).

---

[1]The Tagalog word equivalent to "farm laborer" is not used. Instead they are called *"manggagapas"* (reaper) and *"manananim"* (transplanter).

The farming and non-farming households in the village together provide 86 farm laborers, among whom are included those who usually work in Manila but return to the village in the farming season, for example, the three sons of Felipe Moreno (No. 34).

Farm laborers from outside the village consist of seasonal migratory workers from outside the Municipality of Baliuag as well as members of farming and non-farming households in neighboring barrios and the *kalsada*. These workers organize labor gangs and contract for farm work. Collective migratory workers, such as *sakada* found in the sugarcane plantations on Negros Island and those from the Ilocos region, are not found in this area, but the writer has observed in Kabukiran two groups of migratory workers from other municipalities who take advantage of the seasonal lag in the farm work between different areas. One group consisted of eight members (three men and five women) from Barrio Inaon, Municipality of Pulilan, and two members (two men) from the Municipality of Samal, Province of Bataan. They were engaged in planting for the *dayatan,* staying at the house of their relative's in the village for three weeks in July. This group regularly comes to the village for planting of the *dayatan* and harvesting of the *panag-araw*. The other group consisted of two men and one woman from Barrio Maasin, Municipality of San Ildefonso. They, too, stay at the house of their relative's, and are engaged in harvesting work for about one month in February, together with a group of Barrio Suliban. They come to the village every year.

As mentioned in the previous section, such hired labor is organized into groups which, led by *kabisilya,* contract for planting and harvesting work. Groups for planting work[2] are comprised mainly of women and teen-age boys,[3] while most members of groups for harvesting work are adult male workers; thus the former are generally distinguished from the latter.

As for planting work groups, there are one in Barrio Kabukiran, one in Barrio Suliban, one in Barrio Kalantipay, three in Barrio Telapayong, two in Barrio Pagala, three in Barrio Tangos, and many in the *kalsada*. The groups are engaged primarily but not always in work within their own village. For *dayatan* in 1964, for example, the groups from Suliban, Tangos, Telapayong, and the *kalsada* (Barrio Concepcion) came to Barrio Kabukiran, and the group in Kabukiran worked in Kalantipay. The

---

[2]There is no generic term for this group used in this region; *manananim, kabisilya,* or *upahan* (hired labor) is used as occasion demands.

[3]Adult males are rather ashamed of being engaged in transplanting.

membership of groups ranges usually between 20 and 30, but sometimes exceeds 100.[4]

The principal occupations of *kabisilya* are varied and include cultivators, farm laborers, peddlers, and housewives. Cultivators call on *kabisilya* and designate the time and date of work. Then the latter search for adequate workers and organize them into groups, adjusting the work schedule of each group. Wage rates are agreed on among *kabisilya* at the outset of the farming season; in *dayatan* of 1964, for example, wages for transplanting by the *ordinario* method per one *cavan* (of seeds; equivalent to 1.25 hectares) were 30 pesos,[6] and those for transplanting by the *masagana* method 50 pesos. Lunch is prepared by the workers themselves, and the cultivators provide only coffee, tobacco, and sweets. *Kabisilya* deduct for themselves 3.5 to five per cent of the payment and divide the rest by the number of workers and distribute an equal amount of money to each worker. *Kabisilya* are entitled to one worker's share of wages when they themselves are engaged in planting work. It is estimated that in one season the 35 member group usually transplant seedlings into 35 to 40 hectares of paddy fields for *dayatan* and 75 to 80 hectares for *panag-araw*.

The planting work group in Kabukiran was organized in 1964 by Mauro Gonzales' (No. 31) wife who is usually called by the name of Aling Maming. She became a *kabisilya* and called in the *mananamim* in the neighborhood, who until 1963 had belonged to a group led by a *kabisilya* who lived outside the village. The newly organized group has a membership of 24 (14 men and 10 women) including 10 migratory workers from the Municipality of Pulilan and the Province of Bataan mentioned before; on the average 20 members are daily engaged in work. In 1964, they transplanted seedlings into paddy fields in Barrio Kabukiran and its neighboring barrios for 23 days from July 7 to 29 (for 10 days they worked only a half day). The total acreage of paddy fields they worked was about 40 hectares.

Now let us estimate how much workers get paid for such work. Since the standard amount of labor needed for transplanting one hectare is

---

[4]Such a large group are divided into three teams when they work in the fields.

[5]They were 25 pesos in 1963. Wage rates also differ from village to village; so when seedlings are transplanted in Barrio Pinagbarilan, they are 30 pesos. The reason why such differences in wages exist is not clear; *kabisilya* decide wages among themselves, taking into account the condition of paddy fields and the economic situation of farming households.

[6]P.1=U.S.$0.256. See General Notes 4.

estimated at seven to eight man-days,[7] one worker's daily wages come to 2.90 to 3.30 pesos. How much did one member of the Kabukiran group receive for his 23 days' work in practice? The following equation yields 46 pesos: [30 (wage per cavan) −1 (deducted by *kabisilya*]×1/1.25 (converted into hectares)×40 (number of hectares)×1/20 (per capita). It is safe to conclude that the average worker received 40 to 50 pesos for less than one month's work.

Next we will calculate how much harvesting workers get paid. Groups of harvesting workers are also led by *kabisilya*. In the village there are several *kabisilya* such as Pablo Villanueva (No. 6), popularly called Mang Ambo, who organize their own groups. Mang Ambo's group consists of nine members (seven men and two women), including his two sons and a son-in-law. The units of wages are different for *dayatan* and *panag-araw*. Wages for *dayatan* are one-sixth of the harvested crop for both reaping and threshing work, whereas those for *panag-araw* are seven cavans (five cavans for reaping and two cavans for piling up bundles of palay into *sipok* and *mandala* stacks) for 1.25 hectares. In other words, the wages for *dayatan* are based on the amount of palay harvested, whereas wages for *panag-araw* are based on the area of the paddy fields harvested. Based on his observation that harvesting *panag-araw* crops in one hectare of paddy fields requires 18 man-days,[8] the writer estimates one worker's daily wages at about eight gantas; since the price of one cavan is about 14 pesos, the daily wage would equal four to four and a half pesos.

The work of *bunot,* or pulling and bundling seedlings before transplanting, is also performed by hired labor. Since the wage rate for this work is 12 pesos per hectare, and three to four man-days are required, one worker's wages would be three to four pesos.

[7]*Rice Production*, p. 7.

[8]In the case of Mang Ambo's group, it took six days for nine workers to harvest three hectares.

CHAPTER VII

Land Tenure

1. Types of Tenancy

In Barrio Kabukiran there are 22 landlords, whose relations with tenant farmers including both those who live in the village and those who live outside the village are shown in Fig. 5. The landlords are broken down by number of tenant farmers as follows: two landlords rent to 10 and more tenant farmers each; two landlords rent to between five and nine; 11 landlords rent to between two and four; and seven landlords rent to only one tenant farmer. On the other hand, the tenant farmers are broken down by number of landlords they rent land from as follows: six tenant farmers rent land from two; and the remaining 58 tenant farmers rent land from only one landlord. Of the total 70 cases involving the 64 tenant farmers, there are only 26 cases in which tenant farmers' relations with their present landlords date back to before World War II. Of the remaining 44, there are 30 cases in which landlords changed but tenant faremrs have been farming the same land since before World War II, and there are 14 cases in which both landlords and tenant farmers have changed since World War II.

There are many cases in which relations between landlords and tenant farmers are overlapped by kinship. The relations between Ireneo Rico and the Tolentino brothers (No. 13 and No. 14), between the Corpus sisters and all their tenant farmers in Barrio Kabukiran and Barrio Telapayong, between M. Salvador on the one hand and Nestor Abello (No. 38) and Pedro Cortes (No. 4) on the other, and between B. Jaime and J. Guzman are examples of such relations. Tenant farmers who rent land from landlords who are their relatives do not necessarily pay smaller rents than do other tenant farmers. In the case of the Tolentino brothers who pay 50 per cent of their crops as well as half of their farming expenses, their rents are higher than those of many tenant farmers who rent land from non-relative landlords. On this matter, Tomas Tolentino (No. 13) stated: "Since my landlord and I are relatives, I hesitate to propose changing the terms of the contract. On my part I would like to pay rent in the form of *buwis,* but since I know the landlord does not like that

Fig. 5. Landlords and Tenants in Kabukiran (1964)

Tenants living in Kabukiran	Area(ha)	Landlords	Area(ha)	Tenants living outside Kabukiran

2 A. Corpus — 5.0
15 M. Dizon — 1.5 → R. Corpus (Kabukiran)
32 L. Dalisay — 5.0 — S. Cruz (Baliuag)
    3.0 — M. Menesis (S. Luis, Pampanga)
    3.0 — unknown (S. Simon, Pampanga)
13 T. Tolentino — 1.0
14 R. Tolentino — 2.0 → I. Rico (Baliuag)
25 P. Castillo — 1.3
27 M. Isidro — 1.3 → M. Roldan (Baliuag)
42 D. Hilado — 1.3
    2.5 — C. Cruz (Sto. Cristo)
    1.0 — R. Cruz (Suliban)
    2.0 — Guillermo (Pinagbarilan)
44 L. Hilado — 1.0
16 P. Araneta — 2.5 — P. Feliciano (Baliuag)
    1.0 — N. Gaston (Baliuag)
24 A. Hilado — 1.0
    2.1 — D. Cruz (Suliban)
    2.0 — M. Galvez (Sto. Cristo)
    2.0 — Artemio (Sto. Cristo)
18 A. Mendez — 3.0 2.5
31 M. Gonzales — 3.0 — H. Callastes (Baliuag)
    — A. Saez (Baliuag)
    1.3 — S. Marcelo (Concepcion)
29 R. Sanchez — 2.5 — B. Jaime (Baliuag)
    2.8 2.5 — C. Samson (Baliuag)
    A. Concepcion (Manila)
    0.7 — J. Guzman (Sto. Cristo)
    2.5 — P. Kapanas (S. Simon, Pampanga)

11 G. Corpus — 1.5
20 A. Sanchez — 1.5 // M. Ocampo (Meycauyan)
23 P. Marcos — 2.5 Ⓝ V. Robles (Telapayong)
30 L. Adeva — 1.5
    1.0 — R. Villafuerte (Suliban)
    2.5 — D. Santiago (Concepcion)
    2.5 — J. Pulintan (Suliban)
    2.5 — L. Sanmateo (Sto. Cristo)
    1.3 — B. Andan (Concepcion)
 1 S. Serrano — 1.0
 3 A. Dizon — 1.0
 4 P. Cortes — 2.5 → M. Salvador (Quezon City)
 7 D. Villanueva — 2.0
    1.0 — D. Bernardo (Pagala)
    2.5 — A. Hernandez (Concepcion)
    1.5 — R. Sanpedro (Concepcion)
37 J. Bonoan — 2.5 // R. Balagtas (Quezon City)
38 N. Abello — 2.5 Ⓝ P. Acuña (Tarucan)
    F. Santos (Pinagbarilan)
    2.6 — S. Victor (Suliban)
 6 P. Villanueva — 2.5
17 R. Castillo — 1.2 ++++++ A. Ramoy (Quezon City) ++++++
    0.8 — C. Cruz (Concepcion)
43 E. Hilado — 2.5 1.0 // M. Candido (polo)
    Ⓚ T. Angeles (Concepcion)
41 M. Hilado — 1.5 — B. Laxamana (Pulilan)
26 J. Alonzo — 1.3
39 R. Manahan — 1.5 → J. Gonzales (Manila)
    1.3 — D. Cruz (Telapayong)
    2.0 — N. Roque (Concepcion)
    1.5 — R. Santos (Pinagbarilan)
    1.8 — G. Robles (Telapayong)
34 F. Moreno — 3.5 // P. Tan (Manila)
36 L. Sison — 2.5 Ⓚ E. Carillo (Concepcion)
35 A. Soriano — 2.5
21 S. Serrano — 1.5 // A. Casanova (Quezon City)
22 P. Serrano — 1.9 Ⓚ R. Chico (Sta. Barbara)
28 E. Gonzales — 3.5 — J. Lontas (Manila)
    Roman Catholic Church (Manila)
    Ⓝ B. Carlos (Baliuag)
    1.3 — B. Malonso (Malolos)
    1.3 — L. Sunga (Suliban)

Legend:
——— 1
++++++ 2
══ Ⓚ 3
══ Ⓝ 4

Remarks: 1. *Kasama* relation. 2. *Buwisan* relation. 3. *Katiwala*. 4. *Namumuisan*.
Place of residence is in parentheses.

form of rent I cannot ask him to accept *buwisan*. An advantage in this relationship is that I need not pay any interest when I borrow money from him."

Farm Rent

As in other rice-growing villages, the most common relations between landlords and tenant farmers in Barrio Kabukiran are those based on crop-sharing. It must be noted that in such relations both landlord and tenant farmer are called *kasama*.[1] In a few cases, fixed rents called *buwis* are paid either in cash or in kind; such relations are called *buwisan*. In no case is a lease written; all leases are verbal contracts. The contents of such contracts are described below.

(i) Crop-sharing

First, we shall see how farming expenses are shared by landlords and tenant farmers. Land taxes are all paid by landlords, while tenant farmers pay all the expenses for plowing with the use of tractors and animals, harrowing, and weeding. Expenses for seeds, transplanting, harvesting, threshing, irrigation, and fertilizers are shared equally by both landlords and tenant farmers. It is a common practice in the Philippines for landlords to pay all the land taxes, but it is not so common to go halves on expenses for irrigation, as is practiced in Kabukiran.

Portions of crops are set aside to cover expenses for harvesting (wages for reaping and piling up bundles of palay into *mandala*) and threshing, as well as for seeds to be sown the next season. Then certain percentages (usually 45 to 50 per cent) of the remaining crop are paid as farm rents. Forms and rates of farm rent are tabulated in Table 19.

It is not clear why the different rates of farm rent are prevalent in the village. But we can observe a tendency for the 45 per cent rate to become more common than the 50 per cent rate. At the same time, however, the existence of the different rates reflects differences in sharing farm expenses between landlords and tenant farmers. For example, a landlord, M. Salvador, had exacted the 45 per cent rate until 1961 but has raised the rate to 50 per cent since 1962 on the condition that he would share expenses for planting work. On the other hand, Felipe Moreno (No. 34) pays only 30 per cent of his secondary crops as rent for part of the land

---

[1] *"Kasama"* has been generally understood to mean "share tenant," e.g., K. Pelzer, *Pioneer Settlement in Asiatic Tropics* (New York, 1945), p. 92. In this region, however, *"kasama"* is used in the original sense of Tagalog word, "partner". In this sense, the landlord, too, is actually called *kasama* in relation to his tenant.

Table 19. Forms of Rent (February 1964)

	Number of tenants	Number of landlords and *namumuisan*
Share rent		
60 per cent and over	1	1
50 per cent	24	7
45 per cent	40	12
30 per cent	1	1
not available	3	2
Fixed rent *(buwis)*	2	1
Total*	71	24

* Figures of total are different from the actual number of tenants, and landlords and *namumuisan*, because those who are under two tenancy contracts are counted twice.

Source: Field survey by the author.

which he rents from Pereglina Tan and 45 per cent of his regular crop as rent on the full area. In the former case Moreno pays all farming expenses. Another tenant farmer, Miguel Isidro (No. 27), had his farm rent increased from 45 to 50 per cent in 1961 on the condition that he could borrow money up to 50 pesos free of interest from his landlord. The highest rate of farm rent is paid by a tenant living outside the village, M. Menesis, who farms three-hectare land rented from Segundo Cruz. Menesis pays 50 per cent of his crop as rent for half the land and 75 per cent for the other half, or an average of 62.5 per cent for the three hectares. Menesis says that he is forced to pay such a high farm rent because he owes a large sum of money to his landlord. The same land was farmed from 1961 to 1963 by Lorenzo Dalisay (No. 32), who paid the 75 per cent farm rent in addition to paying all farming expenses. He did this to repay his late father's debt. So we can conclude that paying an extraordinarily high rate of farm rent is a form of repayment of debt and should be regarded in a different light than the ordinary landlord-tenant relation.

(ii) Fixed Rent

In the village there are only two tenant-farmers who have *buwisan* relations with landlords based on fixed rent. They are Ricardo Castillo (No. 17) and C. Cruz living outside the village who rent land from Apolonia Ramoy of Quezon City. Castillo pays 20 cavans of palay a year as *buwis* to Ramoy for 1.2 hectares of single-crop paddy fields and one hectare of residential lot. Taking into account the fact that there are three mango trees around Castillo's house, although rent is not usually paid for residential land, Castillo's *buwis* can be calculated as 14 to 15 cavans per hectare. If the average crop is about 50 cavans, his farm rent is equivalent to about 30 per cent of the crop, with the condition that he bears all farming expenses. The *buwisan* relations in connection with this land were established in 1958 when Ramoy became the owner. Ramoy comes to Barrio Kabukiran only once or twice a year to inspect her land. Like other landlords who live far away and yet do not hire *katiwala,* Ramoy has adopted the fixed rent to avoid the bothersome task of direct management. Ten tenant farmers who rent land from Mauro Ocampo of the Municipailty of Meycauyan paid the 45 per cent farm rent to a *namumuisan* until the summer of 1964, but since the *dayatan* harvest of that year they have been supposed to pay the *buwis* at the annual rate of 20 cavans per hectare directly to the landlord. This case will be treated in detail later. All told by the end of 1964, 12 cases would be *buwisan* relations out of the 71 landlord-tenant relations in the village.

Since 1933 laws for the regulation of tenancy in rice-growing areas have been repeatedly legislated in the Philippines,[2] and these laws assumed Central Luzon primarily as their target areas. It is a well known fact, however, that the laws exercised little regulatory power in practice. The Republic Act No. 1199 called The Agricultural Tenancy Act of 1954 classifies, on the basis of average crops for the preceding three years, paddy fields into first class land (yielding more than 40 cavans) and second class land (yielding less than 40 cavans). The Act further provides that crops be shared on the basis of prescribed rates which are supposed to reflect the respective contributions of production elements, i.e., land, labor, farm implements, work animals, final harrowing of fields immediately before transplanting, and transplanting. Since tenant farmers in Barrio Kabukiran usually pay all the expenses for labor, work animals, farm implements, and final harrowing, and pay half the expense for transplanting, they are entitled to 57.5 per cent of the crops from first class land and 62.5 per cent of crops from second class land. Furthermore, in view of the fact that they pay half the charges for irrigation which should be paid entirely by landlords, and pay the expense for plowing with tractors in the dry season, they are entitled to a still greater share of the crops.

[2]TAKAHASHI, "Land Reform," pp. 314-332.

We can say that the actual rate of farm rent exceeds the legal rate by 2.5 to 7.5 per cent in first class land, and by 7.5 to 12.5 per cent in second class land. The 50 per cent farm rent rate paid by tenant farmers of M. Salvador, however, may be regarded as equal to the legal rate if charges for irrigation water are left out of account, for the land is second class and the landlord pays the expense of transplanting.

Most villagers in Barrio Kabukiran know that the prevailing rates of farm rent are higher than the legal rates, but they also are aware that they cannot demand strict observance of the legal rates in view of the existing power relations between landlords and tenants.

Katiwala and Namumuisan

Katiwala and namumuisan are intermediaries between landlords and tenants as mentioned in Chapter IV. It is customary for landlords who live in the Municipality of Baliuag or its neighboring municipalities to manage directly their land in Barrio Kabukiran. However, absentee landlords who live in distant places depend on katiwala or namumuisan (Table 20 and Fig. 6).

Katiwala is a farm-overseer[3] employed by a landlord. He is remunerated, usually on commission, supervises tenants, and collects rents from them. In many cases one of the tenants is appointed. Katiwala who oversee the land in Barrio Kabukiran are R. Chico of Barrio Santa Barbara (in charge of 3.4 hectares of land owned by A. Casanova), E. Carillo of Barrio Concepcion (in charge of 8.5 hectares of land owned by P. Tan), and T. Angeles (in charge of 3.5 hectares of land owned by M. Candido). All three of these katiwala are tenant farmers who live outside the village and they seldom come to the village except during harvest time.[4]

On the other hand, the namumuisan is a sort of leaseholder who has the character of an intermediary landlord, but not of an agricultural entrepreneur. He is similar to what K. Pelzer mentioned as inquilino.[5] He obtains the right to manage land from a landlord in return for the fixed rent, but the relations between him and the tenants are kasama relations, so that we may say he intervenes in the existence kasama relations between parasitical landlords and tenants like a revenue farmer who collects farm

[3]On the contrary, "farm managers" are those who work for the large size estates and live on salaries.

[4]The tenant farmers did not know how much remuneration these katiwala were being paid.

[5]Pelzer, p. 92.

Table 20. Types of Farm Management by Landlords

	Landlords living in Baliuag	Landlords living outside Baliuag	Total
Direct Management	10	6	16
Katiwala	—	3	3
Namumuisan	—	3	3
Total	10	12	22

Source: Field survey by the author.

Fig. 6. Types of Tenancy

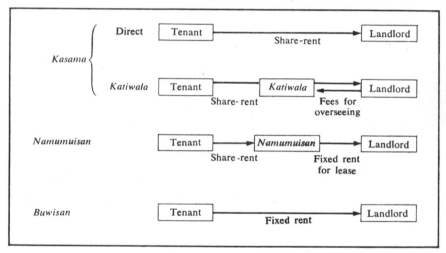

rents for the landlords.

There are three *namumuisan* in Barrio Kabukiran in February 1964. One of them is P. Acuña of Tarucan who rented seven hectares of land from R. Balagtas of Quezon City for the *buwis* of 200 cavans a year. He collects the 50 per cent farm rent from three tenant farmers, paying half the farming expenses. The tenants can borrow money without interest from Acuña. Formerly this land was owned by N. Gaston until 1960 on the direct *kasama* relations between him and tenants. The land was resold from hand to hand, and when Balagtas became landlord in 1962, Acuña who acted as *ahente* in the transaction accepted the post of *namumuisan* for Balagtas.

The second is V. Robles of Barrio Telapayong who became a *namu-*

muisan of Mauro Ocampo of the Municipality of Meycauayan who bought 18 hectares of land in the village in 1961. Until 1960 the land was owned by R. Gonzales and N. Gaston with the direct *kasama* relationship. Robles was formerly *katiwala* for Emilio Rustia. When Ocampo bought Rustia's land at the same time as he got land in Barrio Kabukiran, Robles became Ocampo's *namumuisan*. Robles collected the 45 per cent farm rent from tenants, paying half the farming expenses, while he paid an annual *buwis* of 25 cavans per hectare. In February 1964, Robles demanded that the landlord lower the *buwis* to 20 cavans on the grounds that he was losing because of the high *buwis*. When the latter refused to meet his demand, he planned to raise the rate of farm rent to 50 per cent. When all the tenants refused to pay the higher rate, Robles resigned as *namumuisan*. Ocampo did not appoint a new *namumuisan* and instead demanded that the tenants pay all farming expenses and also pay directly to him a *buwis* of 20 cavans per hectare, beginning with the *dayatan* of 1964. The tenants, however, insist on continuation of the *kasama* relations.

The third is Viuda de Carlos, *arrendador* of the *mitra*. She pays the *buwis* of 6,000 pesos to the archbishop in Manila and collects the 45 per cent farm rent from tenants, paying half the farming expenses (see next section).

2.   Landlord-Tenant Relations

The Tagalog word equivalent to landowner is *"may ari ng lupa"*, but in this region *"propiyetaryo"*, a corruption of a Spanish word propietario which literally means man of property, is generally used for a landlord or landed family. Since land owning is deeply connected with social prestige, that is, to own real estate, particularly farm land, is the necessary qualification to acquire a higher social status, it is easily understood that the word, man of property, became a synonym of landlord. On the other hand the tenant farmer is usually known by the name of *"kasama"* (partner in land cultivation), but the same word also designates the other partner, namely the landlord. Practically, the tenant farmers call themselves *"magsasaka"* or *"magbubukid"*, both of which literally mean peasants.

In the preceding section we have described tenurial conditions from the standpoint of the contract between landlord and tenant. In this section, how the tenant farmers are related with their landlords in actual farm operations will be examined.[6]

Intervention of Landlords in Farm Operation

It is said that in rural villages of the Philippines landlords very often intervene in the farm operation of tenant farmers. The writer often observed cases of such intervention by small-scale landlords in other places in Central Luzon. In Barrio Kabukiran, however, he has hardly ever seen landlords providing their tenant farmers with advice on the selection of varieties of palay, plowing, manuring, weeding, or other farming matters. Asked who determined the plowing method, work schedule and method, and hiring of wage workers, a majority of villagers answered that decisions on such matters were made by the tenant farmers themselves. Landlords rarely visit their land except during harvest time. Of course there are exceptions such as S. Cruz who invested capital to turn his single-crop land into double-crop and who always goes his rounds giving instructions on farming to his tenants. Generally speaking, however, decisions on farming matters are entirely up to the tenant farmers themselves.

When it comes to harvesting, however, it is customary for landlords, *namumuisan,* or *katiwala* to designate dates and methods of threshing, to be personally present at the site of threshing, and to receive rents on the spot. For the threshing of *panag-araw* crops, *telyadora* are often brought in by landlords.

Disputes between Landlords and Tenants

As the landlords' position overpowers that of the tenants economically, socially and politically, it is needless to say that tenants can hardly relieve the pressure of the tenurial conditions under present circumstances. For that reason, cases of tenant farmers' resistance against landlords are not many, but, for all that, a few examples were observed in Barrio Kabukiran.

One example concerns the effort of tenant farmers in the church-owned *mitra* to eliminate an intermediary landlord. As metnioned earlier, a *namumuisan* (called *arrendador* in this case) obtained profits as intermediary landlord by concluding *kasama* relations with the tenant farmers and *buwisan* relations with the Church. When the *buwisan* relations between arrendador Viuda de Carlos and the Church expired in 1963, a parish priest sought the post of *arrendador*. Learning of the priest's intention, about 50 tenant farmers attempted to do away with exploitation

---

[6]Relations regarding social aspects will be dealt with in Chapter XII.

by the intermediary landlord by organizing a farmers' union (*samahan manggagawa*) under the leadership of a local political leader who lives in Barrio Suliban. Making contact with the Office of the Presidential Assistant for Community Development and the Agricultural Productivity Commission, the union filed with the Office of Agrarian Counsel[7] in the provincial capital in June 1964, a petition that "in accordance with the Agricultural Land Reform Code of 1963 (Republic Act No. 3844) we want to discontinue the *kasama* relations with the *arrendador* and instead become leaseholders who will pay the fixed rents (25 per cent of average crops)[8] directly to the landowner." The tenant farmers paid farming expenses for *dayatan* of 1964 and said that they would resort to force to prevent the *arrendador* from collecting rents at harvest time.

It could not then be predicted how the dispute would be resolved, but it is worth noting that the tenant farmers are calling for the abolition of exploitation by intermediary landlords, if not of the landlord system itself, and for the establishment of *buwisan* relations. Furthermore, the tenant farmers are taking positive action to push their demands. Their action is significant in two respects: first, it is opposition to the priesthood which has been at the apex of the power structure in the rural Philippines for the past several centuries, and second, it has drawn support from the Agricultural Land Reform Code.

It must be admitted that the case mentioned above is rather exceptional. In many cases, tenant farmers' protest against the resumption of land by landlords, or their demands for a reduction of farm rents or for a change from *kasama* to *buwisan* relations are squashed by landlords.

Let us examine the case of P. Mendoza who lived in Barrio Kabukiran until February 1964. Formerly he lived in Barrio Kalantipay, renting three hectares of land. When his landlord asked him to return one hectare of land in 1956, he refused the request on the ground that he would not be able to make a living from the remaining two hectares of land. He even brought the matter before the Court of Agrarian Relations on the advice of a leader of the peasants' movement in Baliuag. When the court rejected Mendoza's appeal, the landlord took over all three hectares

[7] The Tenancy Mediation Committee was reorganized into the Office of Agrarian Counsel in accordance with the Agricultural Land Reform Code of 1963. This office acts as proxy for a tenant farmer when he brings his dispute with a landlord before the Court of Agrarian Relations.

[8] When the Agricultural Tenancy Act of 1954 was partially revised in 1959, this rate was determined, but most tenant farmers do not know about the revision of the act.

of land and expelled him from his residential lot. As a result Mendoza came to Barrio Kabukiran in 1959 with the help of his friend, Tomas Tolentino (No. 13), and worked as an agricultural laborer living in a vacant house until 1964 when he left the village to live in other barrio under a new *kasama* relation.

As mentioned before, Tomas Tolentino (No. 13) had rented land in Barrio Pinagbarilan since the time of his grandfather. When the land changed hands in 1954, and he was asked by the new landlord to return the land, he brought the matter before the court. According to him, the court approved his right to grow only *dayatan,* and two years later he gave up farming the land without being paid *puesto* (see next section), for he could not make ends meet by growing only *dayatan.* Until he rented land from a relative in 1960, he was forced to work as an agricultural laborer.

Cases which are brought before the court, like those mentioned above, are few in number, but there are many instances in which tenant farmers who have learned about the Agricultural Land Reform Code of 1963 and have asked that their relations with landlords be changed from *kasama* to *buwisan* relations have had their land taken over on the ostensible reason that the landlords would farm the land themselves. There are also instances in which tenant farmers have succeeded in changing, their relations with landlords from the *kasama* to the *buwisan,* but later have been forced to ask the landlords to revert to the former *kasama* relations because of discriminatory treatment by the landlords. All these instances demonstrate how powerless the tenant farmers are before their landlords. Many tenant farmers mutter that "The Court of Agrarian Relations can do nothing, but *propiyetaryo* can do anything they want," or "It's up to the landlords to decide how the Agricultural Tenancy Act and the Agricultural Land Reform Code should be enforced."

3.   Tenurial Legislations and *Puesto*

Legislation and Tenancy

Before World War II the general rate of farm rent in Barrio Kabukiran was 50 per cent of crops when farming expenses were equally shared by landlords and tenants. It is said that about 1955 the rate of 45 per cent made its first appearance. At about the same time, the once exorbitantly high interest rates began to drop somewhat. The Huk uprisings, which may be regarded as the acme of the peasants' movement in the Philippines, as well as legislation in the social programs of President Magsaysay to cope with social unrest, may be counted among the key factors which brought about these changes. One can hear tenant farmers jokingly saying, "In the previous uprising the rate of farm rent dropped from 50 to 45 per cent. If the next one occurred, it would drop to 40 per cent." The writer has scarcely heard villagers talk about the Hukbalahap and the HMB except in the third person, and yet they seem to think that if the present landlord-tenant relations are slightly better than before World War II, the change has been brought about by the Huks. A majority of them, however, do not seem to expect much from the Agricultural Tenancy Act or the Agricultural Land Reform Code.

Most tenant farmers know that their present shares of crops in the *kasama* relations are smaller than are provided for by the Agricultural Tenancy Act of 1954, but they do not have any correct knowledge about the provisions concerning different shares of crops based on different classes of land and on different contributions of farming expenses. All they know about such provisions is that they are entitled to 70 per cent of crops if they pay all farming expenses. The Agricultural Land Reform Code of 1963 enacted by President Macapagal aims at change from share tenancy to leasehold relations as a preliminary step to establishing owner-cultivatorship as the basis of agriculture. But most tenant farmers' knowledge about the law is a very limited; they know that their tenurial status would be changed from *kasama* to *buwisan,* but they do not know the procedures required for the change or how the amount of *buwis* should be determined. Activities of governmental agencies to publicize such programs are still limited in scope.

It must be stressed that under present circumstances the change from crop-sharing to fixed rent would not mean the complete liberation of tenant farmers from the heavy loads of share-tenancy.

In the first place, even when the fixed rent has replaced crop-sharing, the amount is determined in most cases not in accordance with the provisions of the law but by the arbitrary will of landlords. A tenant farmer's comment that "we are grateful to the Agricultural Land Reform Code for enabling us to establish the *buwisan* relations, but if the landlords raise the amount of *buwis* we shall not be able to pay it," indicates not only his lack of knowledge concerning the legal limit for *buwis* (25 per cent of the average normal harvest [Sec. 34]), but also his helplessness and resignation before the power of the landlords.

Secondly, the fixed rent in the present situation of unstable agricultural production means the avoidance of risks on the part of landlords, but not stable growth of farm income for tenants. The previously mentioned opposition of M. Ocampo's tenant farmers to the introduction of *buwisan* relations and their insistence on the continuation of *kasama* relations (Chap. VII, Sec. 1) are understandable only when this point is taken into account. Since the double-crop land they farm yields about 100 cavans per hectare annually, the *buwis* of 20 cavans comes to about 20 per cent of their crops, and the increase of farming expenses to be borne by the tenants is estimated to be equivalent to about 15 to 20 per cent of the annual crops. Thus the burden on the tenant theoretically would be a little smaller than the previous farm rent of 45 per cent. Besides, in view of the fact that *namumuisan* find their business profitable when they pay the *buwis* of 20 cavans, we cannot say that the tenant farmers of M. Ocampo would not make any profit when they pay the *buwis* of 20 cavans. The tenant farmers, however, argue that *buwis* imposes a greater burden on them than does *kasama* because the amount of their crops fluctuate considerably from year to year. Their argument is understandable, moreover, if we take into account the facts that the tenant farmers can hardly obtain credit from sources other than landlords and that they will have to pay a large amount of interest on borrowed money if they pay all farming expenses.

Thirdly, the tenant farmers fear that if they, as *buwis* tenants, increase the productivity of the land, then the landlords will arbitrarily raise the amount of *buwis,* and it is not unreasonable to believe that the form of rent will revert to a form of share rent again. Thus, we cannot but say that *buwis* is a fixed rent in form but retains crop-sharing characteristics, and we cannot expect that *buwis* will provide tenant farmers with an incentive for investing more capital in land or for increasing agricultural productivity.

When we consider the facts mentioned above, we must conclude that the present *buwis* is essentially different from leaseholding in the modern sense. The change from *kasama* to *buwisan* relations in this area is not necessarily a step forward for tenant farmers, unless it is supported by their own demand for the change as was shown by the tenant farmers in *mitra*. The plight of tenant farmers described in the Bell Report[9] would

[9]"The Philippine farmer is between two grindstones. On top is the landlord, who often exacts an unjust share of the crop in spite of ineffective legal restrictions. . . . Beneath is the deplorably low productivity of the land he works. . . . The incentive to greater production dies aborning when . . . an unjust share . . . goes to the landlord." (U.S., Dept. of State, *Report to the President of the United States*

remain almost unchanged even if the so-called "fixed rent" prevailed. In July 1964 the Municipality of Plaridel adjacent to Baliuag was proclaimed as the first Land Reform District by the President, and efforts have been being made there to establish leaseholders under the administration of the Regional Land Reform Committee. Even in the district, however, basic features outlined above must be far from eliminated.

Puesto

When tenant farmer 'A' wants to give up farming for one reason or another, he announces that he wants to "sell the *puesto* of land" he farms. A prospective tenant farmer 'B' expresses his will to "buy the *puesto* of land," and negotiates with tenant farmer 'A'. If the two parties reach agreement and obtain the consent of the landlord,[10] tenant farmer 'B' pay a certain amount of money to tenant farmer 'A' and becomes the new tenant on that piece of land.

As seen above, when a holding under tenancy changes its cultivator, money is often paid to the former tenant by the new tenant, and the right which realized the payment of the money is called *puesto*.[11] The practice concerning *puesto* is an interesting phenomenon when we study the present land tenure in the Philippines. Since hitherto there has been no detailed report on *puesto*,[12] it will be described in some detail.

(i) *Cases in which puesto was paid.* When Lorenzo Dalisay (No. 32) became a tenant of three more hectares of land owned by Segundo Cruz, he paid 300 pesos[13] per hectare as *puesto* to the former tenant, Berling of Barrio Concepcion. Berling is now working as a carpenter. In another case, G. Robles, who lives outside the village, farms 1.8 hectares of land owned by Joaquin Gonzales. He bought the *puesto* of the land from the former tenant, D. Sison of Barrio Tiaong, in 1964 when the latter moved to Manila. The money paid was 1,300 pesos and covered the price of farm implements. *Puesto* was also paid, although the amounts of money is not known, when Nestor Abello (No. 38) and Pedro Cortes (No. 4) succeeded F. Santiago and P. Matunan, respectively, as new tenants.

---

by the *Economic Survey Mission to the Philippines* [Washington, D.C., 1950], Philippine Book Co. edition p. 63.)

[10]In most cases landlords used to give such consents.

[11]The Spanish word *puesto* means place, position or post.

[12]A similar practice called *pamata* or *postura* was reported in the Province of Pangasinan by Allen. But, unlike *pamata* or *postura*, puesto is usually not paid or received by landlords directly. See Allen, 63.

[13]This amount was approximately worth 77 dollars. See General Note 4.

(ii) *Cases in which puesto was not paid.* Tomas Tolentino (No. 13) once rented and farmed land in Barrio Pinagbarilan, but had a dispute with his landlord when the latter took over the land. The Court of Agrarian Relations mediated the dispute but Tolentino gave up farming the land because the solution did not satisfy him. He was not paid any *puesto.* Later, in 1963, when Ireneo Rico, a relative of his wife, bought land in Kabukiran, Tolentino was allowed to rent that land without paying *puesto.* The former tenant of this land living in Santo Cristo is now a pedicab driver. Domingo Villanueva (No. 7) also did not pay *puesto* when he succeeded his father as tenant.

(iii) *The attitude of landlords.* When the ownership of land changes hands, a new landlord sometimes replaces a former tenant with a new one after paying *puesto* to the former tenant. But more often he takes over the land without paying *puesto* to the former tenant on the ostensible grounds that the landlord himself will be personally engaged in farming. On the other hand, a landlord always declines to pay *puesto* when his tenant wants to return the land to him, and under such circumstances the tenant often looks for a new tenant from whom he will receive *puesto.*

(iv) *The value of puesto.* The average *puesto* is 400 to 500 pesos per hectare of double-crop land and 200 to 250 pesos per hectare of single-crop land; these figures are about seven to eight per cent of the price of land.

The *puesto* is not an old practice and even today it is not a universal practice. However, *puesto* involves several important points. Above data are not sufficient to determine fully the character of *puesto,* but we shall examine further what *puesto* implies.

When a new tenant pays *puesto* to a former tenant, the landlord sometimes acts as intermediary. In principle, however, the landlord never pays *puesto* himself. In this regard *puesto* is different in nature from compensation for removal in the usual sense. *Puesto* is a kind of premium for a farming right, but it is realized only when old and new tenants negotiate directly with each other, or, to put it in other words, only when a prospective tenant appears who is willing to pay *puesto* to farm the land vacated by the outgoing tenant. It is not established yet as a tenant right or right of lease, for it cannot be asserted against the taking over of the land by the landlord. One tenant farmer's comment that "around 1930 there was an abundant supply of land and *puesto* did not exist" suggests that *puesto* has derived from the strong demand by a large reserve of tenant farmers for land in Central Luzon.

The keen demand for tenantable land is a factor sustaining high farm rents and even capable of leading to higher rents. However the Agricultural Tenancy Act and the opposition of tenant farmers make it difficult for landlords to increase farm rents further. Under such circumstances, *puesto,* recompense for acquisition of the privilege of renting land, is paid not as a part of ordinary rent but as a lump sum. At present a landlord acts as intermediary in the payment of *puesto* from a new to a former tenant. But with the *puesto* practice becoming more universal, in the future it is likely that a new tenant will pay *puesto* to his landlord when he succeeds a former tenant and the landlord will pay severance money to his former tenant. Further, it is likely that the *puesto* will come to exceed the severance money, so that the landlord will, in fact, receive a premium payment in addition to the regular land rent. Thus it is possible to assume that *puesto* is an embryonic form of a premium for the farming right.

CHAPTER VIII

Farm Economy

1. Farm Receipts and Indebtedness

How much farm produce do tenant farmers retain after paying farm rents and expenses? As an example of the tenant farmers who belong to the highest-income group, let us examine the case of demonstration farms in a project sponsored by the Agricultural Productivity Commission in

Table 21. Farm Income and Expenses on Three Demonstration Farms, 1962–63 (Per Hectare)

Demonstration farm[1]	A	B	C
Variety of palay	*Wagwag*	*Intan*	*Binato*
Yield (cavan)	78.00	86.25	45.00
Market price (peso/cavan)	13.80	13.00	11.50
Gross income (peso)	1,076.40	1,121.25	517.50
Cost (peso)			
1. Seed (selected out)	12.50	12.50	12.00
2. Seedbed preparation	5.62	5.62	5.62
3. Field preparation	75.00	75.00	75.00
4. Transplanting[2]	40.00	40.00	25.00
5. Fertilizer	34.95	34.95	24.75
6. Weed control	20.00	20.00	20.00
7. Pest control[3]	13.50	8.00	—
8. Harvesting	65.20	52.00	29.21
9. Marketing	3.90	4.30	22.50
10. Irrigation	12.00	12.00	—
11. Incidental	12.00	12.00	—
Total	284.67	276.37	214.08
Net income (peso)	791.73	844.88	303.42

Remarks: [1]The location of demonstration farms: A=Barrio Tarucan, Baliuag; B, C=Barrio Sabang, Baliuag.
[2]Method used: A, B=masagana; C=ordinary.
[3]Insecticide: A=Folidol; B=Endrine.

Source: ARIS Office.

the Municipality of Baliuag. Their accounts are given in Table 21. Needless to say, the level of farm management of these demonstration farms is considerably higher than that of the average farmer in the neighborhood. Since their farming expenses per hectare are 210 to 280 pesos, their income before paying farm rents to the landlord is 800 pesos for *panag-araw* and 300 pesos for *dayatan*. If the income is shared equally by the tenant and the landlord, the former's net income will be 400 pesos for *panag-araw* and 150 pesos for *dayatan*.

It is difficult, however, to think that tenant farmers in Barrio Kabukiran earn such high incomes. Table 22 gives an estimate of an average farmer's income in the village calculated on the assumption that he harvests 50 cavans per hectare for single-crop or *panag-araw* and 35 cavans for *dayatan*, following the standard method of farm operation. Since his expenditure is underestimated, it is safe to assume that the tenant farmer's net income is some two to three cavans lower than estimated. If his share of crops is estimated at 13 cavans for single-crop or *panag-araw* and 10 cavans for *dayatan*, his income in terms of cash is 182 pesos for single-crop or *panag-araw* and 120 pesos for *dayatan*. In short, the tenant farmer's reward for farming one hectare of land using his own working animals and farm implements is only 182 pesos for single-crop or *panag-araw* and 120 pesos for *dayatan*.

Even if tenant farmers could keep this share of the palay crops for themselves, many farming households would be far from self-sufficient in the supply of rice. Since the average size of households is 5.2 members and the annual per capita consumption of palay is six cavans,[1] the average household consumes 31 cavans per year; in order to obtain the net share of 31 cavans, the household needs to farm 1.4 hectares of double-crop land or 2.4 hectares of single-crop land. It is natural, therefore, that households which farm small plots of land, or large households, cannot secure enough rice for their own consumption. It is estimated that 11 of the 36 farming households in the village are substantially not self-sufficient in the supply of rice from their own holdings.

---

[1] According to an estimate by the Food and Nutrition Research Center, Manila, daily consumption of rice per capita in Luzon as average between 1957 and 1962 was 305 grams. Another government agency estimated annual consumption of cereals per capita in 1965-66 as 125.3 kilograms. (B. Bategui and J. Sumagui, "The Food Supply Situation in the Philippines, CY1965-66," *Statistical Reporter*, XI-4 [1967], 11-22.) Those figures are equivalent to 3.9 and 4.3 cavans, respectively, as annual consumption in palay. But villagers in Kabukiran say that six to seven cavans are needed. In view of the fact that villagers have hearty appetites for rice at each of the three meals, this amount does not seem to be unreasonable.

Table 22. Standard Farm Income and Expenses of an Average
Tenant Farmer (per Hectare)

	Single-crop or Panag-araw	Dayatan
(1) Total crop	50 cavans	35 cavans
(2) Crop withheld as expenses		
a. Seeds[1]	0.8 cavans	0.8 cavans
b. Wages for harvesting workers[2]	5.6 cavans	
c. Threshing	2.4 cavans	5.9 cavans
d. Sub-total	8.8 cavans	6.7 cavans
(3) Cash expenses to be shared with landlord		
a. Irrigation fee	12 pesos	—
b. Fertilizers	20 pesos	—
c. Wages for planting workers[3]	30 pesos	30 pesos
d. Wages for workers doing seedling preparation	12 pesos	12 pesos
e. Sub-total	74 pesos	42 pesos
f. Above sub-total converted into palay[4]	5.4 cavans	3.5 cavans
(4) Amount of crop subject to sharing by landlord and tenant farmer[5]	35.8 cavans	24.8 cavans
(5) Farm rent[6]	16.1 cavans	11.1 cavans
(6) Tenant farmer's share of crop[7]	19.7 cavans	13.7 cavans
(7) Cash expenses paid by tenant farmer		
a. Meals and refreshments for *palusong* workers for plowing and leveling	20 pesos	20 pesos
b. Plowing or harrowing by tractor[8]	40 pesos	—
c. Sub-total	60 pesos	20 pesos
d. Above sub-total converted into palay	4.3 cavans	1.7 cavans
(8) Tenant farmer's net income	15.4 cavans	12.0 cavans

Remarks: [1]One cavan of seeds per 1.25 hectares.
[2]For *panag-araw*, seven cavans for reaping and stacking per 1.25 hectares and five cavans for threshing of 105 cavans with *telyadora;* in *dayatan*, one-sixth of crops for harvesting and threshing.
[3]Thirty pesos per 1.25 hectares, and six pesos for refreshments.
[4]Fourteen pesos per cavan of *intan*, and 12 pesos per cavan of *binato*.
[5]$(4) = (1) - [(2) + (3)]$
[6]Forty-five per cent of (4)
[7]$(6) = (4) - (5)$
[8]Either 35 pesos for plowing or 30 pesos for harrowing, and incidental expenses.

Source: Derived from survey findings by the author.

Not only do many farming households lack sufficient rice for their own consumption, but they repay their debts to landlords and merchants in kind, for repayment is necessary to attain new credit for next cultivation. It so happens that some farming households are left with little or no palay at all after paying farm rents and repaying debts.

Some examples in this survey will be given below to illustrate how much farm produce tenant farmers retain.

(i) Paulino Araneta (No. 16) holds a comparatively large area of land. He harvested 112 cavans for *panag-araw* in February, 1964, on 2.5 hectares of land. Since he did not use any fertilizers, and cash expenses on planting and other items were already paid (he did not need to borrow any money from his landlord to pay farming expenses because he had cash income from *karitela* driving), 91 cavans (the total crop minus 21 cavans covering expenses for seeds and harvesting and threshing labor) were subject to sharing between him and his landlord. After paying the 45 per cent farm rent, his share was 50 cavans. After repaying his debts acquired in previous years, he could retain 15 cavans, but since he needed at least 16 cavans for consumption by his three-member family until the following harvesting time, and some portion had to be kept to entertain the *palusong* workers, he could not afford to sell any palay on the market.

(ii) Domingo Villanueva (No. 7) is a medium size tenant farmer. He harvested only 36 cavans for *dayatan* of 1963 on two hectares of land. Six cavans were subtracted from the total crop as farming expenses (the landlord paid planting expenses), and he paid the 50 per cent farm rent out of the remaining 30 cavans. He also repaid a part of an old debt, so that finally he could retain only eight cavans, all of which his household consumed. For *panag-araw* in February, 1964, he harvested 54 cavans on 1.5 hectares of land. After 14 cavans were subtracted from the total crop as farming expenses, his share was 20 cavans, but after repaying his debts, he could not retain any.

(iii) Further down the ladder of stratification, Tomas Tolentino (No. 13) harvested only 37 cavans in February, 1964, on one hectare of land. His share was 16 cavans after five cavans were subtracted from the total crop as farming expenses and he paid the 50 per cent farm rent. He retained only six cavans after repaying his debts to the landlord and did not sell any palay on the market.

(iv) Daniel Hilado (No. 42) harvested 37 cavans for *dayatan* of 1963 and 58 cavans for *panag-araw* on 1.3 hectares of land and retained 10 and 18 cavans for *dayatan* and *panag-araw*, respectively, but since his family consists of 11 members, the rice was exhausted quickly by the large household.

(v) Lorenzo Dalisay (No. 32), the largest tenant farmer in the village, harvested 164 cavans in February, 1964, on five hectares of land, but after repaying half his debts he could not retain any rice at all. On this matter his *kasama* landlord told the writer, "Since he owed me money, I did not allow him to retain any of the crop, and yet he could not repay all his debts to me."

The above examples suffice to show situations in which little or no rice is left for the tenant farmers and their families. This means that almost all the farming households in the village have to meet their living expenses until the next harvest, as well as farming expenses for next season, by cash income from side jobs, by money borrowed from landlords, or by the sale of palay stocked originally for households consumption. They are forced to buy rice on the market once they have sold their own. Both in the selling and the buying of rice the tenant farmers are exploited by intermediary merchants, and they suffer further large losses due to seasonal fluctuations in the price of rice. What is more, they have to pay interest on borrowed money to buy rice. Thus, the tenant farmers have to bear a triple burden (middleman's profit, unfavorable price fluctuation and high interest) because of their inability to produce and keep enough rice for their own consumption.

Since tenant farmers have almost no palay to sell commercially on the market but rather are forced to buy most of rice for their own consumption, not the producers' but the consumers' price of rice is the matter of greatest concern to them. The ratio of farm income in the farming household accounts is so small that the tenant farmers cannot continue farming unless they find sources of non-farm income. Such is the extent to which farming households in Barrio Kabukiran have been alienated from land.

Indebtedness

Under such circumstances in most cases the tenant farmer can earn through farming only a portion of their necessary expenses, not to mention the value of the farm labor contributed by himself and his family. On the other hand, non-farm income is usually not adequate to meet living expenses, so that the tenant farmers are enforced to borrow money to maintain their livelihood and pay farming expenses. Sources from which the farmers can get credit are: (1) governmental agencies, (2) rural banks, (3) city banks, and (4) landlords and moneylenders.

(1) Governmental agencies: The Farmers' Cooperative Marketing Association (FaCoMa) serves as an agent at the municipality level for the Agricultural Credit Administration[2] to extend credit to farmers. It is the primary function of FaCoMa to extend credit to farmers in accordance with contracts on sales of their products. FaCoMa has an organizational network and a large warehouse in the Municipality of Baliuag, however, its officials were involved in a case of alleged malfeasance in 1964, and its activities has been virtually suspended.

(2) Rural banks: There are a relatively large number of rural banks in this region, at least one in every municipality. The rural bank in Baliuag was established in 1956 by a landed family in the municipality.[3] On July 31, 1964, its paid-up capital was 228,000 pesos, and it had outstanding loans totaling 641,000 pesos. The bank provides credit to both farmers and merchants. The number of farmers who received loans from the bank totaled about 1,500 in July 1964, but the amounts of the loans were small, with most of them in the 200 peso range. Once they repay their loans, farmers can raise the amounts of the loans when they borrow the second time. The interest rate is 12 per cent per annum in accordance with the legal regulation, but the actual rate becomes somewhat higher than the legal rate. When Sixto Serrano (No. 1) borrowed 250 pesos, the net loan was 215 pesos after 12 per cent interest and other fees were subtracted from the total loan. In accordance with regulations the bank does not accept real estate as mortgage but demands that landlords or equally reliable guarantors stand as joint surety for borrowers, and its examination of borrowers' credit is strict. As the regulations do not approve repayment in kind, repayment must be made in cash. Seldom do farmers fail to repay their loans. The bank's president has remarked that in the early days of the bank there were some dishonest farmers who did not repay their loans when the loan period expired, but to put them behind bars in jail for a day or two was enough to make them chaneg their mind and behave themselves.

A large number of cultivators in Barrio Kabukiran borrow money from the rural bank. Although data was not available on the exact number of such borrowers, it was found that out of 12 households random-sampled 10 households were in debt to the rural bank. The amounts of

[2]The Agricultural Credit and Cooperative Financing Administration (ACCFA) was reorganized into the Agricultural Credit Administration when the Agricultural Land Reform Code of 1963 was enacted.
[3]This family owns 84 hectares of land in Baliuag and in San Ildefonso, and part of the land is sub-divided for sale as residential land.

these loans were in the range of 200 to 300 pesos. Raul Manahan (No. 39), Barrio Captain (Chairman of Barrio Council), however, had borrowed a large sum of money, 550 pesos, although the size of land he farmed was small. This was possible because he had obtained the confidence of the bank because he had borrowed and repaid punctually for many years. The bank itself admits that 200 to 300 pesos are not sufficient as agricultural funds, and even cultivators who can get loans from the bank seek other sources to borrow money from.

(3) City banks: The Philippine National Bank and the Republic Bank have branch offices in the Municipality of Baliuag. Historically the former used to be one of the biggest sources for agricultural credit in the Philippines, and even today it extends agricultural credit, holding real estate on mortgage. However, it is a bank dealing exclusively with landlords and has nothing to do with small farmers.

(4) Landlords and moneylenders: Eventually most tenant farmers have to borrow money for both livelihood and farming expenses from landlords and moneylenders (usorero). Landlords are the most common sources of funds for tenant farmers, and describe themselves in such an expression as "We are like fathers of tenant farmers."[4] In general landlords lend money at interest, and the interest rate is determined with one harvesting season as the unit period, as in days before World War II.

Today most tenant farmers borrow cash rather than palay or cleaned rice from landlords. Even when they need food, they borrow cash and then go to the market to buy food with it. However, it is common for tenant farmers to repay both principal and interest in palay, and even when they repay the principal in cash, they usually repay the interest in palay. The ordinary interest rate is two to three cavans of palay or 30 to 45 pesos on the principal of 100 pesos. Thus the annual rate is 60 to 90 per cent. When principal is repaid in palay, the price per cavan is usually estimated about one peso lower than the producers' price. When rice is borrowed, the common practice is to repay three cavans of palay on the principal of one cavan of cleaned rice (equivalent to two cavans of palay), or at the rate of 50 per cent interest per half a year. This method of borrowing and repayment is called talindua. The common practice before World War II was called takipan, borrowing and repayment at the rate of 100 per cent interest per half a year, but this practice has disappeared from the scene today. The interest rate for cash bor-

---

[4]The reason why the landlord gives a loan to his tenant farmer even if he is hardly repaid in full will be discussed in Chapter XV.

rowed from moneylenders is usually 10 per cent per month.

When landlords lend money to tenant farmers, interest usually is not demanded if the money is used for such farming expenses as planting, but usually interest is demanded if the money is used for non-farming expenses. The landlord-tenant relationship regarding this matter is greatly varied. In many cases when the terms of tenancy are more unfavorable than average, no interest on loans is demanded by landlords. For example, Tomas Tolentino (No. 13) can borrow money without interest from his landlord because the latter is his relative, but his terms of tenancy are unfavorable in that he has to pay the 50 per cent farm rent and to go halves with his landlord in farming expenses. On the other hand, Miguel Isidro (No. 27) used to pay 10 per cent interest per half a year on money borrowed from his landlord, but the landlord raised the farm rent from 45 to 50 per cent in exchange for the condition that Isidro could borrow up to 50 pesos without interest from him.

Because there appears to be little possibility of producing surplus crops, once a farming household runs into debt the vicious circle of working to repay old debts but being forced to incur new debts seemingly never ends. The large indebtedness of tenant farmers to landlords helps to keep the terms of tenancy unfavorable for the tenant farmers. It is not difficult to imagine how much the tenant farmers suffer from their indebtedness to the landlords. This writer once had casual conversations with four tenant farmers on a footpath, and when the subject of debt was broached, all four complained interminably about it. Some of the farmers' complaints are quoted here. "The moment we begin farming, we get into heavy debt." "We can repay only part of our debts when we have good crops, but when crops fail, we cannot repay any of our debts while interest piles up. *Utang na utang!* (Debt and debt!)" "There is no way of keeping out of debt." "If we repay our debts at harvesting time, we will have to borrow money to buy food the following day. *Utang na utang!*" "Crops in paddy fields never increase, while the cost of living and the prices of animals and fertilizer keep rising. However hard you may work, you cannot get out of debt." "Although we began to harvest two crops a year, all the increase in crops are taken away by *propiyetaryo* because of our indebtedness to them and there has been no improvement in our living." "*Utang na utang!* However hard I may work, my debt keeps increasing. As long as I am in debt, there will be no improvement in my living."

2.   Marketing of Products

How rice produced in Barrio Kabukiran is distributed and marketed is shown in Figure 7. The largest portions of the crops are stored in landlords' warehouses as landlords' shares of crops, as repayments for tenants' shares of farming expenses which were paid by landlords, and as repayments of tenants' debt. Palay is also used to pay for the use of *telyadora,* threshing machines, which are owned by landlords or *propiyetaryo,* and for agricultural wages which are paid to farm workers and peasants who live outside the village. Palay left in the village is part of tenant farmers' shares of crops (frequently these shares are nought as we have seen in the preceding section) and portions of agricultural wages. Since palay left in the village is barely sufficient for farming households' own consumption, tenant farmers never sell palay on the market except in an emergency. The amount of rice left in the village is difficult to measure exactly, but it is obviously very small. In many other rice-growing areas large bamboo containers called *bari* for storing palay are seen quite commonly, but in Barrio Kabukiran only a few *bari* are found. Instead two or three jute sacks containing palay may be found on the kitchen floor of a cultivator's house.

On the other hand, landlords usually store palay in warehouses attached to their houses and sometimes ask rice mills to store it, paying custody charges of 50 centavos per cavan per year.[5] By watching closely the fluctuations in the price of rice on the market, the landlords are able to sell palay to rice mills or rice merchants when a favorable opportunity presents itself.

In the Municipality of Baliuag there are 22 rice mills equipped with a type of rice-cleaning machine called "cono." As a matter of fact, Baliuag leads other municipalities in Central Luzon in the number of such cono mills. The mills clean not only palay produced in the municipality but also palay brought from the Province of Nueva Ecija. Cono mills are large in scale and have the capacity to clean 100 to 300 cavans of palay a day. Owners of rice mills are rice merchants or big landlords.[6] As much as 90 per cent of the cleaned rice is shipped to Manila, while

[5]When landlords sell palay to the rice mill, they need not pay custody charges. When they deposit it at rice mills, one cavan of palay is counted as 46 kilograms, but when they withdraw it, one cavan is counted as 45 kilograms; the subtracted one kilogram accounts for the natural loss in weight.

[6]Different from other areas in the Philippines, Chinese is not playing significant role in rice milling in this municipality.

Fig. 7. Flow of Rice

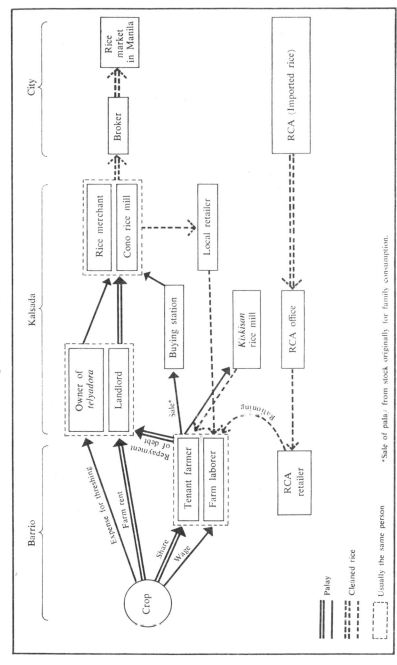

*Sale of pala; from stock originally for family consumption.

Palay

Cleaned rice

Usually the same person

the remainder is sold by retailers in the local markets to consumers, including peasants.

Peasants sell palay through a different route than do landlords; they sell rice to small brokers, called buying stations, who in turn sell it to rice mills. These buying stations, which total more than 20 in number, spring up on the fringes of the *kalsada* at harvest time. Since buying stations, unlike rice mills, specialize in buying small quantities of rice, peasants can sell palay with one kilogram as the minimum unit. However, buying stations buy palay 40 to 50 centavos cheaper per cavan than do rice mills.

The price of palay varies according to varieties and quality, and its seasonal fluctuations are also great. Generally speaking, the price of palay is highest in May and June, the off-crop season; it drops a little bit with the early harvesting of *dayatan* in August, and is lowest in September and October (*dayatan* harvest) and January, February, and March (*panagaraw* harvest). In 1963-64 the following fluctuations was observed in the buying price of palay per cavan by variety at rice mills. The price of *wagwag* which is harvested in December and January was highest (21 pesos) in October, then dropped to less than 15 pesos in January and February and rose again to 20 pesos in August. *Intan* was 14 pesos in February and increased to 18 pesos in August, while *binato* from the *dayatan* was between 12 and 14 pesos in August and September and rose only a little to 14 to 15 pesos in May and June. In other words, the highest price is from about 10 to 40 per cent higher than the lowest price. The seasonal fluctuations in the price of rice work to the disadvantage of peasants who are forced to sell palay to repay their debts when the price of rice is lowest and to buy rice for their own consumption when the price is highest.

Peasants have palay for their own consumption cleaned at small, primitively equipped mills called *kiskisan*. They buy necessary food items at the market. But as for rice they tend to buy imported rice rather than domestic rice because the latter is expensive. In an attempt to lower the price of rice through the importation of inexpensive foreign rice, the Rice and Corn Administration of the national government set up in every barrio throughout the country an RCA retailer in charge of distributing imported rice in 1964. The *sarisari* store owned by Sixto Serrano (No. 1) has been designated as an RCA retailer, so RCA-administrated foreign rice is rationed to all the villagers in Kabukiran. Such is the actual situation of supply of food in a rice-growing village in the Philippines.

CHAPTER IX

Rural Employment

1. Jobs off the Farm

In the preceding chapter we have observed that cultivators in Barrio Kabukiran produce little surplus and that they cannot support their households unless they are engaged in jobs off the farm. In this section the self-employed side jobs of farming households will be described.

Karitela and pedicab

The horse carriage called *kalesa* which seats two persons, and the horse carriage called *karitela* which accommodates nine persons used to be the most common means of transportation in the *kalsada* and in rural barrios, respectively. Recently the "jeepney," a remodeled jeep whose capacity is 10 persons but into which as many as 20 persons can be squeezed, has begun to be used between the plaza and distant barrios. The number of pedicabs in the *kalsada* has also increased in recent years, while the number of *kalesa* has sharply decreased. The total number of licensed *kalesa* and *karitela* in the Municipality of Baliuag was 115 in July 1964. However, since many horse carriages from the Municipalities of Bustos and San Rafael as well as barrios in the Province of Pampanga come to Baliuag to do business, the Municipal Treasurer of Baliuag estimates the number of operating horse carriages in the municipality at more than 500.

The *karitela* made its appearance in Barrio Kabukiran when the road to the village was completed in 1959. Since the village is at some distance from the *poblacion,* villagers use *karitela* when they go to the market in the *poblacion* or to church, or when they transport farm produce. As of June 1964, there were five *karitela* in the village; all operated by peasants as side jobs. These carriages ply between the village and the plaza two or three times a day. Passengers are not only villagers of Barrio Kabukiran,[1] but also residents in other barrios along the road to the *poblacion.* Usually five or six passengers are found riding on a

---

[1] Almost all the villagers are close relatives of the *karitela* and pedicab drivers, but they pay fares without fail.

karitela. Fares are 20 centavos one way. On Wednesday and Saturday, the market days at Baliuag, the number of passengers is doubled. At harvest time *karitela* ply between the village and the *poblacion* six to seven times a day to accommodate increased traffic as well as to transport the newly harvested palay. In the rainy season, most village households find themselves in straitened circumstances, so most villagers walk to the *kalsada* and the revenue of *karitela* drivers drops. The price of a horse is 350 to 450 pesos and a carriage and its accessories cost 300 to 350 pesos. Such operating expenses as the price of feed and molasses cost one to 1.5 pesos a day. The *karitela* driver's income fluctuates considerably, ranging from three to five pesos a day on weekdays and between five to eight pesos on market days, while at harvest time it soars to as high as 10 pesos a day. Since business is frequently suspended during the busy farming season and the hottest weeks of the year, it may be safe to estimate the net revenue of a *karitela* driver between 1,000 and 1,500 pesos a year.

Each of the five *karitela* drivers in the village was in the same business when he lived in the *kalsada*. Four are relatively large tenant farmers. Rodolfo Sanchez (No. 29), who farms 5.3 hectares of land, continued the *karitela* business when he returned to the village from the *kalsada* in 1959, and at present he owns two horses which alternate drawing a carriage. Paulino Araneta (No. 16), who farms 2.5 hectares of land, had been driving a *kalesa* in the *kalsada* since 1943; when he returned to the village in 1961, he switched to a *karitela*. Lorenzo Dalisay (No. 32), who farms five hectares of land, is the son of a former *kalesa* driver in the *kalsada* who assumed his father's business in June 1964. Pastor Marcos (No. 23), who farms 2.5 hectares of land, began his side business in the *kalsada* about 1947. Jesus Alonzo (No. 26), who farms 1.3 hectares of land, began the side business in the *kalsada* but has suspended it since July 1964.

On the other hand, the number of pedicabs has sharply increased since 1961. The number of licensed pedicabs in the Municipality of Baliuag is 817, but the number actually operating in the municipality exceeds the 1,000 mark. The price of a new pedicab is 500 pesos, and that of a second hand one is 350 pesos, but the price paid on monthly installments is around 100 pesos higher. Most drivers are boys between 14 and 20 years of age; men older than 20 account for only one-third of the pedicab drivers. A large majority of the drivers rent pedicabs from bosses in accordance with either the so-called "boundary" system (paying the fixed rent of about 1.3 pesos a day) or the *pakikilabas* (50 per cent commission). A driver's gross daily income is three to five pesos, but on days of *barrio fiesta,* however, it rises to as high as eight pesos.

Three farming households in the village each own a pedicab. Two of them, Andres Dizon (No. 3), 35 years old, and Miguel Isidro (No. 27), 23 years old, are small tenant farmers farming one to 1.3 hectares of land and are heads of households. In the case of Jaime Bonoan (No. 37), who farms five hectares of land, his second son, 20 years old, is mainly engaged in driving the pedicab. All three are self-employed. Since there are few fares in the village, they work in the *kalsada* most of the time. In the busy farming season, they rent out the pedicabs to their relatives or friends under the boundary system. Their annual income from the business is estimated between 800 and 1,000 pesos.

Stores and Barber Shop

A tiny general store facing the road running in the middle of the village is managed as his side job by Sixto Serrano (No. 1), a tenant farmer who farms only one hectare of land. He is also engaged in a barber's job and in agricultural wage labor. His is the only store in the village where miscellaneous goods for daily consumption are sold.[2] Part of the *silong* is enclosed and shelves are set up, so it is the simplest kind among the so-called *sarisari* stores. Sold at the store are Coca-Cola, cheap liquors, tobaccos, matches, candles, canned food, seasoning, soap, candies, and vegetables, all of them in small quantities. Since the store was designated as an RCA retailer in April, 1964, it has been in charge of rationing one ganta of rice per day to each household in the village. Ordinarily the wife of Serrano attends to the store, weaving *buntal* hats. Serrano buys a stock of goods once or twice a week at wholesalers' stores in the *poblacion* and at the municipal market, and carries the goods home by bicycle. He also earns commission by delivering goods to *sarisari* stores in other barrios and by serving as an errand man for villagers.

The sales at the store are about 10 pesos a day, one half in cash and the other half on credit.[3] Payment for credit purchases is made at harvest time. Compared with *sarisari* stores in other villages, the ratio of credit sales to the total sales at Serrano's store is small. Villagers usually

[2]In April 1965 Manuel Dizon (No. 15) opened a new *sarisari* store utilizing the *silong* of his house. The funds for renovation of the *silong* and for the initial inventory of commodities was raised with aid from the Government Service Insurance System since he is a municipal employee.

[3]Several households in the village have been refused credit.

buy most of their daily necessities when they go to the market in the *poblacion* on market days, so they buy only small miscellaneous things at Serrano's store. Regular customers of the store are limited to about 30 households in the neighborhood. This store does not play any role in the marketing of farm produce.

In addition to managing the *sarisari* store, S. Serrano doubles as a barber. The only fixtures in his barber shop are a homemade wooden chair and a mirror. Being the only barber in the village, he cuts the hair of 20 to 30 persons of Barrio Kabukiran and other neighboring barrios in a week. There are three methods of paying for hair-cut services: cash payment, payment in kind, and labor exchange. The cash payment is 40 centavos per hair-cut. The payment in kind is one cavan of palay per person per year at the rate of one hair-cut per two weeks. The amount of palay Serrano receives as payments for his barber services total 15 to 17 cavans a year. In labor exchange (*batalis*), customers work for Serrano, but there is no fixed form. Serrano's monthly income as a barber is estimated at about 40 pesos. It is interesting to note that such payment in kind still exists in the Philippines, even though the cash economy has spread widely to rural villages.

Besides the *sarisari* store, there is a store called *cantina* managed by Felipe Moreno (No. 34). Located at his own house behind the school, the store sells soft drinks and cheap candies to schoolchildren. Its sales are very small.

Buntal Hat Weaving

Buntal hats, often called Philippine Panamas, are elaborate hand-woven hats whose main material, *uway,* is the leaves of hemp palms produced in Southern Luzon. Being very expensive (15 to 50 pesos apiece in Manila), they are mostly exported to foreign countries. Until the early twentieth century *buntal* hats were one of the most important export goods of the Philippines. Today *buntal* hat weaving is a brisk cottage industry employing female labor in the northern part of the Province of Bulacan and the southern part of the Province of Nueva Ecija. Since the Municipality of Baliuag is the center of *buntal* hat production in the region, a large number of *uway* dealers and hat brokers flock to the market in the *poblacion* on market days. One woman weaves usually one or two hats a week; three hats are the maximum number she can weave within a week. She sells semi-finished hats with no hemming to the brokers. The cost of material is about 1.2 pesos apiece, and the worker earns about five pesos per hat for her labor.

Almost all women above 10 years old in Barrio Kabukiran weave *buntal* hats, using simple tools. Young women have other opportunities for work such as transplanting, but most housewives do not engage in farm work. Except for domestic work, *buntal* hat weaving is the only occupation open to housewives, so it is one of the most important sources of cash income for them. Thus, of the 44 households in the village, as many as 40 are engaged in *buntal* hat weaving. Semi-finished *buntal* hats are brought directly to the market and sold to brokers for cash. There is no subcontracting by wholesalers. Many workers suspend *buntal* hat weaving in April and May because these are the hottest months of the year and because fibers of the material become so dried up and hardened that they become difficult to handle. In the *kalsada* many housewives subcontract to sew garments, but in Barrio Kabukiran this occupation is not found.

2.   Wage Workers

It is a characteristic of rice-growing in the Philippines that even small farmers are heavily dependent on hired labor. In Barrio Kabukiran farming households employ a large amount of wage labor at planting and harvesting times. The demand for agricultural laborers grows acute in each of the four busy seasons of the year. Since the number of agricultural laborers and the amount of their wages have already been mentioned in Chapter VI, here we shall avoid repetitive descriptions and instead focus on five agricultural workers of non-farming households who depend entirely on agricultural wage labor for their livelihood.

Emilio Manahan (No. 40), the elder brother of the Barrio Captain, does not farm any land as a tenant. He is hired as an agricultural wage worker in Barrio Kabukiran and other barrios in the Municipality of Baliuag and sometimes even in the Municipality of San Miguel as the demand for planting, preparation of seedbeds, harvesting, and other farm work arises. He mows grass and sells it as feed to *karitela* drivers, catches fish, and engages in other miscellaneous jobs, while his wife devotes herself to weaving *buntal* hats. Except for one who is sick, his sons also are engaged in agricultural wage labor.

Carlos Corpus (No. 12) farms only 0.25 hectare of single-crop land in addition to helping his uncle Manuel Dizon (No. 15) with farming, thus he depends almost completely on wage labor for his livelihood.

Mario Corpus (No. 8), the younger brother of Carlos Corpus (No. 12), has recently begun to farm part of his uncle Antonio Corpus' (No. 2) paddy fields for *dayatan* in addition to helping his uncle with farming. He is also engaged in growing rice in the *bana,* but in both cases his crops are very small. Agricultural wage labor such as plowing land with the use of a *kalabaw* owned by his uncle Antonio is the main source of his livelihood. In this regard he is in the same situation as his brother Carlos.

Conrado Tolentino (No. 33) worked as a roadman in Manila before World War II. After the war he returned to the village and built his house on a corner of residential land where Felipe Moreno (No. 34), his son-in-law, lives. Conrado Tolentino and his sons are employed as wage workers, while his wife and daughter weave *buntal* hats. The daughter also works as a *manan* *anim.* All the family are engaged in wage labor.

Jesusa Balao (No. 5) is a widow who is living together with her old mother and her child. Both the widow and her mother work as *manananim* in the planting season; aside from this, they weave *buntal* hats all the year round.

There are two household heads who are engaged in non-agricultural wage work.

Manuel Dizon (No. 15) is a clerk at the municipal hall. Graduate of a high school, for 17 years he held a part-time job as a market tax collector working only on market days. In addition he farmed. In December 1963 he became a permanent clerk at the municipal hall and now commutes there on a bicycle. His land is 1.5 hectares in the *bana* and three hectares of land in Barrio Telapayong, all single-crop land. On holidays and after office hours on weekdays, he farms the land, assisted by his nephew Carlos Corpus (No. 12).

Ramon Araneta (No. 19) is a tractor driver. Formerly he helped his uncle Paulino Araneta (No. 16) with farming and also worked as an agricultural wage worker. He learned to drive a tractor while he was employed in a public work project in the Cagayan Valley. Since he returned to the village in 1963, he has been employed by a civil engineering contractor in the Municipality of Baliuag to drive a farm tractor and a bulldozer. He receives one peso per hour. When he finishes his work, he returns home and works as an agricultural wage worker while waiting for his next job. Although he says, "With my driving skill, I can easily find a job," his net working time as a driver is only about three months a year. He rents and farms part of P. Araneta's (No. 16) paddy fields for the *dayatan* only, but his income from the land is small, as in the case of Mario Corpus (No. 8).

Aside from the two household heads mentioned above, those who are engaged in non-agricultural wage labor include a wireman, a sawmill worker, a beautician's apprentice and a store clerk, all employed in the *kalsada*.

The number of workers employed away from home is not large. Three sons of Felipe Moreno (No. 34) work at an automobile repair shop in Manila, but in the busy farming season they return to the village to help their father and also to work as agricultural wage workers. There are two girls who are working in Manila, one as a clerk at a pharmacist's store and the other as a seamstress. As for seasonal migrant workers, there are agricultural workers and carpenters. Agricultural migrant workers from this village go to the Municipality of San Miguel and to the Province of Bataan for planting and harvesting work. The number of such workers totals 12. Arrangements for work are made by their relatives in the respective places. It is said that in former days many villagers in Barrio Kabukiran were engaged in carpentry as side jobs. Today six villagers go to Manila to work as carpenters in the dry season. Usually they are employed as assistants by friends and relatives who are carpenters.

3.   Employment Situations

In Chapter III the occupations of the villagers were described briefly. Here we shall examine the nature of the villagers' employment more closely. Table 23 indicates in what occupations the villagers are primarily engaged, and in what status they are employed. Of the 109 employed persons, 29 per cent are engaged primarily in farming of their own holdings, 19 per cent in self-employed small business and cottage industries, and the remaining 52 per cent in agricultural and other wage labor. Most villagers also are engaged in secondary jobs. The breakdown of secondary jobs is shown in Table 24.

Of the 32 villagers engaged primarily in farming (all of them are tenant farmers), only four are engaged exclusively in farming; one is Antonio Corpus (No. 2), a comparatively large tenant farmer, who has the *comunidado* right; the other three are old people whose ages are 80, 65, and 59. Of the 28 villagers engaged primarily but not exclusively in farming, 26 are employed as agricultural wage workers, and two work as seasonal migrant carpenters.

Table 23. Employment in Kabukiran by Occupational Status (1964)

Employed persons	Male	Female	Total
Self-employed			
Farming	32	—	32 (29%)
Small business	11	2	
Cottage industry	—	8	} 21 (19%)
Employed			
Agricultural wage labor	20	25	} 56 (52%)
Other wage labor	7	4	
Total	70	39	109 (100%)

Source: Field survey by the author.

Table 24. Side Jobs of Employed Persons in Kabukiran (1964)

Main occupation	Side jobs	Male	Female	Total
Farming	None	4	—	4
	Agricultural wage labor	26	—	26
	Other wage labor	2	—	2
Self-employed small business	None	—	—	—
	Farming	6	—	6
	Farming and agricultural wage labor	5	—	5
	Cottage industry	—	2	2
Cottage industry	None	—	8	8
Agricultural wage labor	None	10	—	10
	Farming	10	—	10
	Self-employed small business	—	—	—
	Cottage industry	—	25	25
Other wage labor	None	1	4	5
	Farming	2	—	2
	Farming and agricultural wage labor	4	—	4
Total		70	39	109

Source: Field survey by the author.

Of the 13 villagers engaged in self-employed small business such as *karitela* and pedicab driving, barber, and *sarisari* store, none are exclusively engaged in such business. Six are in farming, five are both self-employed and hired in agriculture. Two women attend to the *sarisari* store and the *cantina,* but also weave *buntal* hats. Eight of the 13 are household heads.

Twenty male villagers are employed as agricultural wage workers; one half of them help the heads of households with farming in addition to working as wage workers, while the other half are employed exclusively as wage workers. The latter group includes not only agricultural workers from non-farming households but also three men who work exclusively as wage workers although they belong to farming households. All of women employed in agricultural wage works are also engaged in weaving *buntal* hats.

Of the 11 villagers who are engaged in non-agricultural wage labor, five, namely a wireman, two store clerks, a seamstress, and a beautician's apprentice, are engaged exclusively in such work. Three of them work outside the village. The remaining six help their families with farming or are employed as agricultural wage workers in the farming season, in addition to being employed in non-agricultural wage labor. The latter group includes Manuel Dizon (No. 15), who is the head of a farming household.

As shown above, the employment structure in the village is complicated; only 27 persons, or 25 per cent of the employed population are engaged in a single occupation, including workers in cottage industries, while the other 75 per cent are engaged in one or two side jobs.

Next, we shall examine where labor force in the village is employed. Five villagers work primarily in Manila. Fourteen villagers leave Baliuag seasonally as agricultural wage workers or as carpenters. Of the seasonal workers, agricultural wage workers who belong to non-farming households and who are engaged exclusively in such labor frequently work outside the village, but others do so only for short periods once or twice a year. The number of villagers who work in the *kalsada* is 16, including *karitela* and pedicab drivers. It may be concluded that most of the labor force in Barrio Kabukiran is employed in the village and its vicinity.

The demand for labor in the village comes from two sources, the agricultural sector and the non-agricultural sector. In the non-agricultural sector only cottage industries and self-employed small businesses as side jobs provide opportunities for work. Consequently the demand for labor comes primarily from the agricultural sector. As has been described in detail in Chapter V, farming in the village is operated by small tenant farmers. The village specializes in growing rice in paddy fields with little attempt made to grow vegetables or raise chickens and swine. Many paddy fields remain single-crop land and land use is not intensive since farm operation is far from efficient. Under such circumstances the demand for labor in the agricultural sector is limited, even though mechanical power is introduced into only a few processes of cultivation and important processes are still dependent on human labor. While even small tenant farmers are dependent on hired labor in the farming season, they cannot adequately absorb their own domestic labor in farm work in the off season. This situation is indicated by the fact that as many as 95 per cent of the farming households in the village are part-time farmers.

Of the employed population of 109 in Barrio Kabukiran, 94 are employed to some extent in the agricultural sector, and 50 out of 94 are self-employed in farming. On the other hand, those who are employed to some extent as agricultural wage workers total 80 in number. In addition, there are 31 households which farm land in the village but live outside the village, and in the busiest season a large number of agricultural wage workers pour into village from other barrios and municipalities, resulting in a large accumulation of labor. Such being the circumstances, it can be assumed that labor in the village is underemployed.

It is difficult to accurately record the numbers of working days and the nature of work of each occupational group in rural areas. As to the employment situations of farming households in the Philippines, statistical findings have been reported by Oppenfeld and others based on an extensive sampling survey.[4] Since the patterns of employment in the village are complicated, data on such matters were obtained at best as rough figures in this survey. Here a brief description is presented based on interviews and observations.

As a model, a head of a farming household who farms two hectares of land will be sketched. He himself is engaged in the following kinds of farm work. (i) Plowing: with the assistance of three men on *palusong* basis, the work is finished in three days. (ii) Harrowing and leveling:

---

[4]The average employment of tenant farmers was as follows: the farm operator worked for 4.9 months on his farm and 2.2 months in off-farm work, and remained unemployed for 4.9 months; the family members worked for 3.4 man-months on the farm and 7.1 man-months in off-farm work, and remained unemployed for 8.7 man-months. See H. Oppenfeld *et al., Farm Management, Land Use, and Tenancy in the Philippines* (College, Laguna, 1957), p. 60.

four days of work with the assistance of *palusong* workers. (iii) Preparing and sowing seedbeds: five days of work. (iv) Pulling and bundling of seedlings: one day spent for supervising hired wage workers. (v) Transplanting: two days spent for transplanting seedlings and for serving refreshments to wage workers. (vi) Weeding, irrigation, and other care in the growing period of palay: one or two days of work a week, or a total of 25 days of work in the four-month period. (vii) Harvesting and threshing: seven days spent for taking care of wage workers hired for the occasion. (viii) Miscellaneous work after harvest: three days of work. Thus, he works on his farm for a total of 50 days; besides, he works in other farmers' paddy fields without remuneration for about 20 days in return for *palusong* labor. If he harvests two crops a year, his total working days will be 140 to 150 days a year. He also spends about one hour a day to take care of his *kalabaw*.

Suppose this household head is also engaged in agricultural wage work as his side job. Since household heads usually do not engage in transplanting work, only harvesting and threshing provide him with opportunities to work for wages. The harvesting period is about 30 days for the *dayatan* and two months for the *panag-araw*, but during each he must spend at least 10 days on his farm. If half of the remaining harvesting period he is available for wage work at most,[5] he can work in other peasant's farms for 10 days for the *dayatan* and for 25 days for the *panag-araw,* or a total of 35 to 40 days for the two harvesting periods. Thus, it is clear that even the household head, who is engaged primarily in farming works on both his own and others', farms for only 180 to 190 days at most. As mentioned earlier, the farming seasons of the year vary according to the date when ARIS begins to supply water for the village. In 1963, preparations of paddy fields were begun in May with the plowing season continuing through planting in June; the period from late August to early October was the season for harvesting *dayatan* and transplanting *panag-araw;* the period from mid-January to early February was the season for harvesting *panag-araw*. The four-month period from late February to June[6] did not see any work at all.

This is a standard model of employment for the head of a farming household in the village. Actually the writer has the impression that the busyness of the farming season in a Philippine rice-growing village is entirely different in nature from that in a Japanese village. When wage

---

[5]This estimate was derived from the observation empirically.

[6]In even-numbered years, start of farming is delayed. See Fig. 4.

workers are hired for transplanting and harvesting work, they are responsible for the work, while the cultivator or his family members play only an auxiliary role; in extreme cases, the head and members of the household remain mere onlookers. It may be said that during the growing season, too, they often are taking it easy.

As for wage workers hired for transplanting and harvesting work, the intensity of their labor is not high. They begin to work at 8 a.m., at the earliest, and often they work for only half a day. Aling Maming's team of *manananim* were hired for 23 days of transplanting the *dayatan* in July 1964, but for about 10 of these days they worked only half a day on the grounds that there was a shortage of seedlings, that harrowing had not been completed yet, that work was finished earlier than scheduled, etc. And even at the time of planting when the farm work is supposed to be busiest in the year, and when *manananim* from other barrios are brought into the village, many villagers get together in front of the *sarisari* store and enjoy gossiping in the daytime. Since most of household heads do not engage in transplanting, they seemed to have time on their hands except when they are engaged in harrowing on the *palusong* basis.

Even in the farming season labor is not fully engaged, as mentioned above. In the slack season from February to June labor is left completely idle. Although villagers say that this season is a time to find jobs as seasonal workers in rice mills and sawmills or in carpentry, very few of them actually do so. As for carpenters, it was first said that 15 to 20 villagers used to work as seasonal carpenters, but interviews with farming households revealed that only six villagers had worked as seasonal carpenters in the previous three years. In 1964 only one villager, the eldest son of Jaime Bonoan (No. 37), earned some income as a carpenter. Others did not work on the grounds of a family member's sickness, of busyness as an officer in charge of the village festival, and so on. Still others gave the following reasons for not working as seasonal carpenters: "I want to work in Manila but I cannot find any job unless I have a friend there"; "Unless you know a master carpenter, you cannot find any job"; "I cannot leave the village because I have to take care of my *kalabaw.*" As for agricultural workers of non-farming households, Emilio Manahan (No. 40) and Conrado Tolentino (No. 33) usually go to Manila and other areas as migrant workers, but others such as the Corpus brothers (No. 8 and No. 12) remain in the village. Of those who remain in the village, only a few try to earn extra income from hunting birds, catching fish, or growing vegetables. A majority of the villagers spend their time chatting and say, "March, April, and May is the period for *pahinga* (rest)."

Life in Barrio Kabukiran in both the farming and the slack seasons has been sketched briefly above. What has struck the writer most strongly is that the peasants seem to minimize their input of labor into the land they hold. This fact will be dealt with in detail in Chapter XIV. Here it should be pointed out that such an attitude of the peasants is understandable in view of the fact that any increase in farm productivity would bring about little increase in farm income for the tenant farmers who have to pay high rates of farm rent and are heavily in debt to the landlords. Thus, a large portion of the labor force in the village is chronically underemployed and seasonally unemployed. The basic reason for such a situation is the deficiency of employment opportunities for the surplus labor force in the village. But at the same time, it should not be overlooked that exploitation by the landlords deprives the tenant farmers of the positive will to expand their effort and attention to their land.

CHAPTER X

Economic Stratification

In the rice-growing region of Central Luzon independent farmers, let alone agricultural entrepreneurs, are rarely found, but instead parasitical landlords hold most of the land. Thus the basic class relations are those between landlords on the one hand and tenant farmers and rural wage laborers on the other. In Barrio Kabukiran, however, no landlords live in the village except for a very small one (most of the land is owned by absentee landlords), and their agents, *katiwala* and *namumuisan*, do not live in the village, either.

Of the 44 households in the village, 42 are households of tenant farmers and agricultural wage laborers, while one is a household of the small landlord and the other is a non-productive household. Though the tenant farmers are holding and operating their farmland, they are deprived of a large share of their crops by the landlords and are increasingly dependent on off-farm works to supplement their farm income. In substance they are being turned into proletariats. What is more, the status of the tenant farmers is very insecure, and the alternation of status between tenant farmers and wage laborers is frequently observed. Thus, a distinct hierarchical demarcation between tenant farmers and rural wage laborers does not exist, but rather the difference between these two strata is ambiguous. It can be said that the economic stratification of Barrio Kabukiran is not characterized by hierarchical order but by horizontal structure. This is the most fundamental characteristic of economic stratification in the village.

With the above fact in mind, let us now examine the economic stratification in the village more closely. The area of cultivated land alone does not constitute a valid indicator of economic strata in the village. The farming households' demands for labor and farming incomes vary greatly, depending on whether the land cultivated is fit for single-cropping or double-cropping. Thus, a large holding of cultivated land does not necessarily mean a large farm income. We will divide the households into different economic strata on the basis of the gross cultivated area, income level, and standard of living; off-farm work and other factors have also been considered in the division.

(1) Upper Stratum: One Household

This household leases its land and receives a small amount of rent. Coupled with the land rent, a pension makes this household the recipient of the largest and most stable income in the village. Sometimes the household loans money to villagers. It should be regarded as a landlord who rents out superfluous land because of a shortage of family labor rather than as a parasitical landlord. (Household No. 9.)

(2) Middle Stratum: Eight Households

These households cultivate relatively large holdings and their farm incomes are larger than those of other farming households. They lead a more or less stable life, with some of them engaged in self-employed businesses. They keep many draft animals. Many village officials come from this stratum.

This stratum is subdivided into two groups. The households in the first group cultivate 5.0 to 9.1 hectares of land, are engaged in *karitela* driving and other self-employed businesses, and have stable cash incomes. Their houses are made of wood and are substantial structures compared with those of other farming households. Some of the family members go to high school. The households in this group are Households No. 16, No. 23, No. 29, No. 34, and No. 37.

The households in the second group cultivate 5.5 to 8.0 hectares of land and are engaged primarily in farming, with their off-farm wage incomes accounting for a relatively small proportion of their total incomes. The three households in this group are Households No. 2, No. 24, and No. 28.

(3) Lower Stratum: 19 Households

This stratum is subdivided into three groups. The two households in the first group (No. 15 and No. 32) derive stable incomes from works off the farm and cultivate large holdings (4.5 to 10 hectares), but because of low productivity of *bana* land and of heavy debt, their farm incomes are unstable.

The 13 households in the second group cultivate average size holdings of land (from 3.0 to 5.0 hectares), but their wage incomes are unstable. They are Households No. 6, No. 7, No. 11, No. 14, No. 17, No. 18, No. 20, No. 30, No. 31, No. 38, No. 41, No. 43, and No. 44.

The four households in the third group cultivate small areas of land (1.0 to 2.0 hectares) and are engaged in self-employed businesses. They are Households No. 1, No. 3, No. 26, and No. 27.

(4) Lowest Stratum: 16 Households

This stratum is subdivided into four groups. The eight households in the first group cultivate small areas (less than 2.5 hectares) and are heavily dependent on wage incomes which are unstable. They are Households No. 13, No. 21, No. 22, No. 25, No. 35, No. 36, No. 39, and No. 42.

There is the only one household (No. 4) in the second group, which cultivates a small holding (2.5 hectares) and whose off-farm income is also small.

The third group consists of the six households of wage laborers whose incomes are unstable. They are Households No. 5, No. 8, No. 12, No. 19, No. 33, and No. 40.

The only household in the fourth group is Household No. 10 which is retired from productive work.

Thus, four strata are recognized in the village, but it should be re-emphasized that hierarchical differences among them are not distinct and that the strata are rather horizontally structured.

The problem of the historical development of economic stratification will be dealt with in Chapter XVI. However here it should be mentioned that this writer tried to trace the economic situations of forefathers of farming households in the village as far back as possible. He could obtain some information on the fathers of the present householders, but he found it extremely difficult to elicit answers to questions on the grand-fathers. So far as the information obtained on the fathers and grand-fathers is concerned, the status of the respondents' fathers and grand-fathers was *kasama* (share tenant). The only exception is Rafael Corpus who has climbed his way from tenant farmer to landed farmer and now even owns land to rent out. In all other cases, the fathers and grand-fathers were *kasama* in the village, or in other places where they had lived before coming to the village. It was impossible to identify the years in which such events took place. But it would seem certain that the dis-integration of landholding had occurred well before the turn of the century.

CHAPTER XI

Social Relations and Political Organization

1. Social Relations

Settlement

Though the agglomerated pattern of settlement is generally common in Philippine villages, Barrio Kabukiran has a rather dispersed pattern. Fifteen houses are clustered in a residential land which is somewhat elevated from the surrounding paddy fields. Aside from this, there are only three places where three or more houses are gathered. All other houses are scattered far and wide in the paddy fields, alone or in twos.

The reason for such a pattern of settlement is that residential land is offered for tenants' use by landlords. Except in the case of several households owning residential lots in the central part of the village, all residential land is rented to tenants free of charges. The landlords allow the tenants to build houses on residential land, or sometimes in parts of paddy fields. The landlords encourage the tenant farmers to live close to their farmland, for it facilitates farm operations. Since the landlords do not allow other villagers than their own tenants to use land free of charges, except when the tenants want to accommodate their relatives within their house lots, the fragmented landholding results in the dispersed pattern of settlement. In this sense the pattern of settlement is a reflection of the pattern of landownership. The dispersal of the three public facilities in the village, school, chapel, and health center, is due to the fact that the land they stand on has been offered by three different landlords. It is worth noting that the village lacks strong unity even in the physical pattern. As for neighboring villages, the agglomerated pattern of settlement has been adopted in Barrio Telapayong where old, large landholding such as *mitra,* account for a large proportion of the land, while in the other neighboring villages the dispersed pattern is prevalent.

Family

It is generally said that in Philippine villages the extended family is common, and in addition to family members it includes one or two extra-

family members.[1] Almost all the households in Barrio Kabukiran, however, are nuclear families. Only two of the 44 households in the village
have two married couples in the same household, and in one of two such
households the elder couple live in a house in the *kalsada* in the slack
season. The size of families ranges from one to 11, most ferquently from
four to seven, and the average size is 5.2 persons.

The nuclear family pattern exists in the village partly because youths
of marriageable age leave the village, and partly because houses are of
such simple construction that new houses for newly-weds are easily built
once the approval of landlords is obtained. In building a bamboo house
with a living room and kitchen, for example, one gets bamboo growing
on the land of his landlord or his relative free of charges or for a nominal
price and enlists the labor services of neighbors in a *batalis* (labor exchange) basis. In the market one has to buy *nipa* worth 50 to 100 pesos
as material for the roof and walls. Including the cost of nails, rattan,
and wires, one can get a new house for about 150 pesos.

The form of inheritance is division of the legacy into equal portions
among siblings, as was earlier illustrated in the case of Rafael Corpus,
the only landowner in the village (Chap. IV, Sec. 2). In reality, however,
the legacy is not actually divided but the six brothers and sisters jointly
own them, each claiming a one-sixth share, even after they have become
independent. Such a form of joint ownership, called *comunidado,* is frequently observed among other landlords. To the other farming households which have nothing but houses and *kalabaw,* inheritance offers no
problem. The case is common in which one succeeds his father as a tenant of the land, or part of the land, which the father cultivated when he
died or retired. In such a case the prior understanding of the landlord
is needed, for the right of tenancy is not established.

Figure 8 shows kinship among the households in the village. There are
seven major consanguineous groups whose members are related on the
fathers' side, while affined relationships are interwined with these consanguineous relationships like a cobweb. The number of households which
are not involved in the network of kinship, including those who have
migrated to the village very recently, is only nine out of the 44 households. Although the high rate of intra-village marriages is a common
phenomenon in Philippine villages, yet the extraordinarily high rate of
such marriages in Barrio Kabukiran may be accounted for by the recency

[1]See, for example, C. L. Hunt *et al., Sociology in the Philippine Setting* (Manila,
1954), p. 88, and Rivera and McMillan, *Rural Philippines,* p. 133.

Fig. 8.   Kinship in Kabukiran

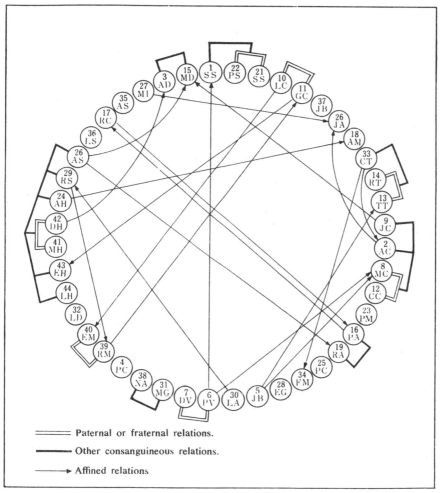

of the village settlement. Affined ties are not concentrated in any particular economic stratum. Nor is any preference given to paternal or maternal relations.[2] We can say that kinship relation is cognatic. Being

[2]This is generally observed among the Catholic people in this country. "In the Philippines, descent is reckoned bilaterally, which means that one is equally related to both his father's and mother's consanguine kin with no preference structurally for either side." (Hollnsteiner, *Dynamics*, p. 64.)

different from the "family constellation" in the Leyte village[3] or from the "*Dōzoku*"[4] relation in rural Japan, there is no socially dominant family which becomes the focal point of family relations in the village.

In addition, many villagers are involved in ritual kinship, as *ninong* (godfather), *ninang* (godmother), *inaanak* (godchild), *kumpare* (compadre) and *kumare* (comadre), based on the Catholic ritual. This *compadrazgo* relationship complicates as well as strengthens family relations. Families related by kinship are closely interdependent on one another in every aspect of social and economic life: labor exchange in the form of *palusong* or *batalis,* lending and borrowing of food and farm implements, offering tenanted land for growing *dayatan* or for making seedbeds, and support in election campaigns. However, such close association with kins does not always mean ambiguity in family tie. As Hollnstein pointed out, primary loyalties belong to one's nuclear family and, by extension, to his other kinsfolk.[5]

Chapel and Fiesta

All the families in Barrio Kabukiran are Roman Catholics; no one belongs to the *Aglipayan* or the *Iglesia ni kristo* sect. As is the case with most barrios in the Philippines, the barrio, an administrative unit, serves also as an ecclesiastical unit. In other words, all the villagers are members of the same *bisita* (barrio chapel). The complete independence of Barrio Kabukiran was given impetus by the movement to build an independent *bisita* in 1955 (Chap. III, Sec. 3). Construction of the *bisita* started in 1955 but has not been completed yet; up to 1964 more than 5,000 pesos, most of which were contributions from the villagers, are said to have been spent on its construction. The cross and a statue of San Roque, the patron saint of the village, are placed on the altar, and benches seating 30 to 40 persons are placed in rows on the floor. On the days of fiesta a priest of the church in the *poblacion* comes to the *bisita* and holds Mass, but ordinarily the *bisita* is not used very much. When one wants to attend Mass on Sundays, one must go to the church in the *poblacion.* Baptism and funerals are also held at the church.

The barrio fiesta (*pista sa nayon*), which is usually held between March

---

[3]"Family constellation . . . refers to a grouping formed with a core family at the center and then its attachments to other families by kinship or by special interest." (Coller, p. 83.)

[4]"*Dōzoku*," literally "common kin," is a lineage comprising a stem family and its branches (not necessarily consanguine of the stem).

[5]*Dynamics*, p. 67.

and May, is the biggest event in Philippine rural life. The whole village makes preparations for the festive occasion. On the day of fiesta villagers open their houses to entertain passers-by, let alone their relatives and friends, as much as possible. It is true that many villagers overspend themselves for entertainment. The story is often told of those who after having been elected officials of the fiesta, such as *Hermano Mayor* or *Matanda sa nayon,* got themselves into heavy debt through overspending. Generally speaking, however, expenditure on the fiesta corresponds to the economic power of each villager, so how the fiesta is celebrated reflects economic and social differences arising from the stratification of the village.

In Barrio Kabukiran the fiesta is usually held in early April; in 1964 it was held on April 4 and 5. Mass is held at the *bisita* and afterwards a procession with the statue of San Roque in the center makes the round of the village. Behind the *bisita* about a dozen booths are set up, and a stage is built in their midst. In the evening several entertainments are performed on the stage, lighted by a diesel power generator. People from the *kalsada* and nearby barrios come to see the festivities, making the occasion the biggest holiday of the year in the village.

To hold the fiesta, three committees are organized every year and they prepare special assignments and provide expenses. Those are the *Lupon ng Katandaan* (committee of seniors, comprising heads of households), *Lupon ng Kabinataan* (committee of bachelors), and *Lupon ng Kadalagaan* (committee of unmarried young women). In 1964 the *Katandaan* paid expenses for the printing of invitation cards to be sent out to neighboring barrios, an honoraria for the Mass, fees for a 17-member musical band for the procession plus meal expenses for them, the price of candles for the procession and rent for lamps, the price of firecrackers, and meal expenses for the eve of the fiesta, totaling all together about 1,300 pesos. The *Kabinataan* paid the rent for a power generator and a loudspeaker, the fees for entertainers, and the cost of prizes, totaling all together about 300 pesos. The *Kadalagaan* paid the expenses for decorating the *bisita,* which totaled about 200 pesos.

Many means are devised to collect funds for the fiesta. There are about 60 households which are members of the *Katandaan,* including some of households which cultivate land in the village but do not live in the village. The members are asked to contribute one cavan of palay cach in the case of a farming household and 10 pesos in the case of a non-farming household, and these contributions amount to about 800 pesos. Each member of the *Kabinataan* is asked to contribute three pesos. Contributions are also solicited by bringing invitation cards to relatives and friends living outside the village. Occasionally a dancing team called *mananuyaw* is organized to collect funds. The team makes the round of nearby barrios and municipalities, performing song and dance shows and thereby soliciting contributions. Landlords are also asked to contribute, and most of them contribute 20 to 35 pesos, although some decline to do so.

The management of the fiesta in this village is not very different from that in other villages, but several small differences emerge if it is closely observed. For one thing, the fiesta in the village is moderate compared with other villages; the merry atmosphere, characteristic of an ordinary fiesta, cannot be said to permeate the village, and the number of visitors from outside the village is not as large as it is in other villages. For another, in striking difference from the custom in other villages, the degree of participation in the fiesta varies markedly from household to household in the village. While Rodolfo Sanchez (No. 29), living next door to the *bisita* and being its custodian, and Felipe Moreno (No. 34) and Jaime Bonoan (No. 37), both fiesta officials, were busy entertaining a large number of guests until late at night and spending large sums of money, many households did not receive any guests nor participate in the procession. It is worth noting that households in the latter group did contribute their shares of the fiesta expenses and some of them were among the fiesta officials. Such a situation must be very peculiar among Philippine villages. From this we may conclude that the villagers of Barrio Kabukiran are not well of economically, since only a few households in the village can afford to entertain guests to the extent which is quite common in other villages. The three households mentioned above are all in the middle stratum as identified in Chapter X, cultivate relatively large holdings of land, and have stable cash incomes from such side jobs as *karitela* and pedicab driving and working away in Manila. Differences between strata are minimal in this village, and yet they are reflected in the way the fiesta is celebrated.

2.   Political Organization

In charge of the politics of the Municipality of Baliuag are a mayor, a vice-mayor, and eight municipal councilors. Occupations of these ten officials include merchant, landlord, and businessman, and nine of them are from the *kalsada*. The tenant farmers' interests are not effectively represented in municipal politics. Villagers in Barrio Kabukiran do not show any interest in politics on and above the municipal level except in elections. The Municipality of Baliuag belongs to the Second Congressional District of Bulacan and is a part of the sphere of influence for a congressman of the Nacionalista Party, who is a lawyer in the Municipality of Santa Maria.

On the village level there is the barrio council comprising a barrio captain and six councilmen, who are elected to four-year terms by popular vote. These barrio councils are autonomous organizations which have existed for a long time, and were officially established by legislation called the Barrio Charter in 1959[6] (later revised in 1963). The barrio council is designated to plan and execute economic, educational, public health, and other programs, and is endowed with taxing power. In reality, however, it serves as the lowest level unit of local administration controlled by the central government.

In the January 1964 election two teams of candidates campaigned in Barrio Kabukiran. Candidates for the post of barrio captain were Raul Manahan (No. 39) and Gabriel Corpus (No. 11), each followed by six candidates for the posts of councilmen. Of about 140 eligible voters, 93 went to the polls. Manahan was elected barrio captain and four of his team and two of the Corpus team were elected councilmen.[7]

Generally, in barrio council election, it is common for different factions based on kinship to fight one another. This writer observed considerable tension in election campaigns in Barrio Virgen de las Flores and Barrio Tiaong. In Barrio Kabukiran the situation looked somewhat different, however. This writer heard a villager say, "Since the former captain, Agustin Hilado (No. 24), declined to run this time, we asked Manahan to run. Then, to make the whole thing look like a formal election, Manahan asked Gabriel Corpus to register as an opposing candidate. Accordingly, there was no ill feeling between the two contending teams of candidates and there was no real campaigning." Although it is difficult to take the villager's account at face value, this writer in his observations did not find any factions existing in the village. What is more, the sister of Raul Manahan is the wife of Gabriel Corpus, and the sister of Gabriel

[6]Before legislation of the Barrio Charter, organization and administration of barrio were provided in the Revised Administrative Code of the Philippines.

[7]The elected councilmen were, in the order of votes obtained, Sixto Serrano (No. 34), Felipe Moreno (No. 34), Pablo Villanueva (No. 6), Arcadio Sanchez (No. 20), Paterno Castillo (No. 25), and Paulino Araneta (No. 16).

Corpus is the wife of Emilio Manahan, brother of Raul Manahan; thus the two candidates are related by a doubly affined relationship.

The captain and councilmen are not concentrated in any particular stratum, and the dates when they settled in the village are different. All of them are graduates of a primary school and one, Sixto Serrano (No. 1), is a high school graduate. Although he was born in the village, Raul Manahan cultivates only 1.5 hectares of land, one of the smallest farms in the village, and supplements his farm income with agricultural wages. He is 36 years of age and among the youngest group of village officials. Villagers interpret that he was supposed as barrio captain on the grounds of working hard for village affairs, having a fluent tongue, and being a good community leader. It would appear that the lack of status hierarchy in the village is reflected in the election of the barrio council.

CHAPTER XII

Village Community

1. The Land System and the Village

As was noted in Chapter VII, the landlord-tenant relations are extremely strict in economic terms, and not infrequently tenants are deprived of almost all the crops they produce, including the value of their labor, by landlords. Besides, the landlord-tenant relations include not only the paying and receiving of farm rents, but also tenants' indebtedness to landlords. But these relations remain purely economic and it is unlikely that landlords dominate the social life in the village. It is true that landlords are asked to contribute toward the village fiesta, and small and medium-size landlords living in the Municipality of Baliuag sometimes give instructions on farm operation to their tenants. But landlords seldom intervene in village politics or in the way of life of villagers.

When landlords and tenants meet each other, there certainly are signs of the tenants being reserved and constrained. Sometimes tenants give small presents to landlords making the round of their land. It is difficult, however, to regard such landlord-tenant relations as those of domination and subordination between persons of unequal status like master and vassals. When landlords loan living expenses to tenants, they refer to themselves as "something like a father of a tenant." To some extent the landlords' attitude is benevolent, but it is a common practice for them to demand interest or charge higher rents than normal in return for loaning money. Thus, non-economic factors are not so significant in the landlord-tenant relations. It is not unusual for tenants to be ignorant of the full names of their landlords. This is the case especially when *namumuisan* or *katiwala* intervene as agents for landlords. Even when landlords live in the same municipality, many tenants do not know much about the occupations, genealogy, and family members of their landlords.

The only landlord living in the village owns a very small size of land in the form of *comunidado*. Since this household is headed by a female, it does not command any influence socially, although villagers consider it as belonging to the upper stratum.

Thus, we may conclude the landlord-tenant relations are very impersonal and usually limited to economic aspects only. It is difficult to conceive that the vertical element of landlord-tenant relations plays a fundamental role in the village society. Such a generalization, of course, is applicable with regional limitations. When powerful landlords live in the village or big absentee landlords station *katiwala* in the village, the landlords and *katiwala* may exert strong influence on social relations and politics as well as on economic relations. Cases in which landlords reinforce economic relations through social and political pressures were observed in nearby villages.

The next question is how the economic status of villagers is reflected in their social positions. It may be assumed that the amount of land cultivated by farming households, or the distinction between farmer and non-farmer, is reflected in the social and political relations in Barrio Kabukiran. All the officials of the barrio council and of the fiesta are heads of farming households, and most of them cultivate comparatively large area of land. It was farming households in the upper and middle strata that pushed the independence of Barrio Kabukiran. However, as was noted in Chapter X, all the farming households are in substance proletarianized, so the amount of land cultivated is no direct indication of economic stratum. Besides, differences between strata are not distinct, nor are differences between farming and non-farming households marked. In this village which is horizontally structured, differences in economic strata result in minimal differences in social positions and do not constitute the status hierarchy. We may say that the village society essentially is based on more or less equal status of villagers.

Finally, we shall look at peasants' organizations. Peasants' unions were once among the most powerful social and political groups in Central Luzon. The first peasants' movement in the Philippines took hold in this area, especially, the movement came to the fore in Pampanga and the northern part of Bulacan. In this region such organizations as *Kapatiran*[1] and KPMP[2] were very powerful and infiltrated into peasantry. In the

[1]*Kapatiran* (literally meaning brotherhood or fraternity) was a group of peasants organized in the late 1920's in Bulacan and Pampanga, which fought against landlords to reduce farm rents. The first tenants' organization in the Philippines, *Pagkakaisa ng Magsasaka* (Farmers' Union), was also organized in the southern part of Bulacan in 1917.

[2]In 1919 the Union de Aparceros de Filipinas (Tenants' Union of the Philippines) was founded, but soon was renamed Confederacíon Nacional de Aparceros y Obreros Agrícolas de Filipinas (National Federation of Tenants and Agricultural Workers of the Philippines). In 1924 it was renamed again *Katipunan Pambansa mg mga Magbubukid sa Pilipinas* (National Union of Peasants in the Philippines) or KPMP, and played a leading role in the peasants' movement especially in

late 1940's the rice and sugarcane zone of Central Luzon, including the Municipality of Baliuag, was one of the hotbeds for the Hukbalahap. Such a movement has been completely subdued by the governmental forces since the 1950's. It is difficult to find out what has become of the movement and how the former activists are faring underground (see Chap. XVII, n. 3). The Bulacan Farmers' Association and the Bulacan Workers' Association have recently been organized in the southwestern part of Bulacan, but they have not been organized as yet in Baliuag. As was mentioned in Chapter VII, a movement to oust an *arrendador* from a *mitra* in an adjacent barrio was begun under the leadership of a local politician. This was the only peasants' movement observed in this Municipality. How a new movement might affect social relations in the village remains to be seen.

2.   Communal Features

Now let us examine communal relations in the village, beginning with communal ownership and use of land. All the land in the village has come under private ownership, so no communal land is left.[3] Some communal relations exist in the secondary use of land, however. For example, peasants who cannot make seedbeds because of the difficulty in obtaining water for their land use other peasants' land free of charge; in such a case landlords do not intervene. It is also the common practice in this region for peasants to pasture their *kalabaw* and cows in paddy fields after the harvest without the permission of owners or cultivators. But when cattle damage standing crops, their owners are responsible for compensation. Peasants are also permitted to mow grass for animal feed and manure even when crops are in the growing season. Cultivators are not entitled to the exclusive use of the grass on the levees in their paddy fields. This writer observed in the municipalities of San Miguel and Gapan that in dry season many tenant farmers allow the use of their paddy fields to others to grow vegetables on a commercial basis, but such a case is not

Bulacan and Nueva Ecija. Later, being united to another peasant group, the AMT, *Aguman Ding Maldeng Talapegobra* (Workers and Peasants' Union), in 1946, this organization became the PKM. *Pambansang Kaisahan ng mga Magbubukid* (National Peasants' Union) and developed into the mass base for the Hukbalahap. See A. Scaff, *The Philippine Answer to Communism* (Stanford, 1955), pp. 10, 153.

[3]At the beginning of Spanish colonization, *tingues* was commonly owned in Tagalog society. (E. H. Blair and J. A. Robertson, *The Philippine Islands 1493-1898,* [Cleveland, 1903-1909]. Vol. VII, pp. 174-175.) The writer understands *tingues* as forest and grass land.

seen in Barrio Kabukiran yet.

Irrigation is considered to be one of the factors fostering communal unity in Monsoon Asia. Can we say this of Barrio Kabukiran? It was in the 1920's that the irrigation system was introduced in this region, and it was done by the government, so to speak, from above. As was mentioned earlier, the management of the irrigation system is in the hands of the government. At the village level, however, anarchy prevails over the use of irrigation water. Although the shortage of water is one of the most serious problems in farm production, the peasants make no efforts at all to exert self-control or to maintain effective use of the irrigation system. On the other hand, it is the established custom for peasants to channel water across other peasants' cultivated land. Sometimes damage is caused by the custom, but it is considered unavoidable. From this we may conclude that no positive measures to regulate the use of water exist within the village, or among villages, but that a sort of pressure is brought to bear on each farming household by the village community.

Now we shall consider labor relations. It is generally understood that labor exchange is the basic form of farm labor in Philippine villages,[4] as well as being a communal feature of the village society. In Barrio Kabukiran, however, farm production is performed primarily by the cultivator's own labor and hired wage labor. Only plowing and harrowing are performed on the basis of labor exchange called *palusong*. Since labor for *palusong* is low in quality because it is offered "for company's sake" (*pakikisama*) and expenses for meals and refreshments for *palusong* labor are by no means small, farming households tend to prefer hired labor to *palusong*. At the present stage *palusong* generally provides labor for plowing and harrowing because expenditure for these operations would be entirely borne by cultivators. There is also another form of labor exchange called *batalis* or *bayanihan,* which is a mutual aid for non-farming purposes.[5] Certainly such forms of labor exchange enhance a peasants' "sense of gratitude" (*utang na loob*)[6] to one another and strengthen bonds of human relations, but communal labor is not a major factor in farm production. In this region hired labor plays the fundamental role in

[4]See, for example. B. M. Villanueva, *A Study of the Competence of Barrio Citizens to Conduct Barrio Government* (Quezon City, 1959), p. 114, and Covar, p. 63.

[5]This form of labor exchange was often observed in reconstruction work, for example, for houses damaged by typhoon. Labor is not immediately repaid but later at a time when the other party needs it.

[6]Literally it means "a debt inside oneself." See M. Hollnsteiner, "Reciprocity in the Lowland Philippines," in *Four Readings on Philippines Value,* compiled by Frank Lynch (Quezon City, 1964), pp. 22-49.

farm production.

Communal features, as reflected in the joint ownership and use of the means of production and in labor exchange, have been considerably weakened, but farming households as units of production have not acquired the initiative in deciding of farm operations as yet. We should not overlook the fact that the village community is putting pressure on each farming household to regulate processes of farm production. Two such examples will be given below.

The first example concerns the division of labor. As we have seen in Chapter VI, processes in growing palay are sharply divided into those performed by family labor and those performed by hired labor. That is, transplanting and harvesting (reaping and threshing) work are performed by workers from both inside and outside the village hired for wages in cash or in kind. It is true that because of low labor productivity family members cannot supply all the necessary labor during the busiest time, but the fact is that wage workers are hired not only to meet the shortage of family labor, but also to follow the custom that planting and harvesting work is in principle performed by hired labor. This custom is socially established and followed by all the farming households. Heads and members of farming households do not play any leading role in the work on the land they cultivate; in planting they may help with leveling paddy fields and carrying seedlings, but in harvesting they never participate at all.

When family members participate in planting and harvesting work, they are allowed to do so as members of the team of hired workers, not as family members of the cultivator, and they receive the same wages in cash or in kind that are paid by the cultivator to the hired workers. Since the participation of family members in this work in their own land means reducing the incomes of neighbors, it is not encouraged. Peasants explain that the custom is designed to give opportunities for income to peasants and wage workers in the neighborhood. It is not unusual for peasants, who cannot afford to waste one cavan of palay, to be away from their own land right in the midst of harvesting time. This means that peasants are creating employment opportunities for one another.

The second example concerns the custom in accordance with which villagers not directly involved in farm production are in practice given some shares of the crops. This takes the form of gleaning, bringing home reaped palay stalks or picking up palay at the site of a *mandala* after threshing. The amounts of palay collected this way would not seem to be large, but closer observation reveals that they are quite considerable.

The method of reaping palay is very rough and a large quantity of palay is left uncut. There is also a considerable amount of fallen ears lost in bundling the reaped palay. Gleaning of this palay is called *pulot,* and a gleaner *namumulot.* Reapers are followed immediately by many *namumulot* who may number 20 to 30 per cent of the reapers. The amount of *pulot* is said to be about one cavan per hectare.

There is another custom of reapers' bringing home a sheaf of palay from among those they have harvested, aside from wages. This custom is called *pumpong,* and those who bring it home *namumumpong.*[7] Such palay is meant for feed or food for families but it can be also sold in the market.

After being threshed by a *telyadora* palay straw is piled up at the site until it is disposed of as feed or manure, and everybody is permitted to glean at such a site. One to 1.5 cavans of palay is said to be collected from the straw from one hectare of paddy field.

Thus, there is a difference between the crop for the landlord and cultivator on the one hand and the actual crop on the other, and that difference is shared by villagers other than the cultivator. As is the case with planting and harvesting work, cultivators and their family members do not participate in such gleaning, in principle.

The custom is accepted with resignation by landlords and landed farmers, who have been heard to say, "The custom means a smaller crop for us, but the custom is the custom. . . ." and "Only those who live from hand to mouth are engaged in gleaning, and it can't be helped. . . ." On the other hand, tenant farmers go somewhere else during harvesting time, as was mentioned above, to "show their trust (*napakakatiwalaan*) in the reapers." As was noted in Chapter VIII, the tenant farmer's share for cultivating one hectare of land is frequently less than 10 cavans of palay. Thus, the fact that two to three cavans of palay is gleaned by other villagers contributes significantly toward reducing the farm incomes of tenant farmers. At first glance such behavior of the tenant farmers seems irrational, but we must remember that their hiring other tenant farmers on one day and in turn being employed by the others on the following day is one way of ensuring their livelihood by increasing incomes from

---

[7] A similar custom was reported in villages in Western Java. During harvest time paddy fields are "opened" to inhabitants both in and outside the village, and everybody (usually female) is allowed to join harvesting work and bring home bundles of rice as wages. Some earn as much as one to two months' food supplies during one harvesting season. UENO Fukuo, *Nōson jittai chōsa hōkoku* (Survey Report on Desa Tjimahi, Soekaboemi, Bogor), (Batavia, 1944), pp. 139-140.

work on land other than their own. Furthermore, this custom tends to share the risk of crop failure on any particular holding among the villagers.

From the two examples given above, we may conclude that some communal pressure is applied on individual farming households and serves as one means of protecting villagers' livelihood against deprivation by landlords, and that although most of the communal features in Barrio Kabukiran have been lost, some remnant features are still at work.

CHAPTER XIII

A Summary of Findings

1. The Municipality of Baliuag is located in the monocultural rice growing zone of the Central Luzon Plain and is the center of commerce and education in the northern part of the Province of Bulacan. It is about 50 kilometers away from Manila, and bus and train transportation makes it possible for inhabitants of the municipality to commute to Manila.

2. Barrio Kabukiran, one of the barrios in the Municipality of Baliuag, is a rice-growing village. Its area is 151 hectares, its population is 423, and the number of households is 44, of which 36 are farming households. The size of farms ranges from one to five hectares, and the average size of farms is 2.5 hectares. Thirty-one farmers of neighboring barrios hold and cultivate farmland within Barrio Kabukiran, and on the other hand, five farming households in Barrio Kabukiran cultivate farmland in other barrios.

3. The history of the village is recent. The increase of population began at the beginning of this century. During the years from 1942 to 1955 most of the villagers evacuated to the town proper to avoid sufferings from both World War II and the Hukbalahap revolt.

4. All the farming households in this barrio are tenants and are at the same time have one or more members engaged in side jobs. The heads of nine households are engaged primarily in side jobs. The number of non-farming households is eight, and six of them are wage laborers.

5. Occupations of the gainfully employed workers in the village is as follows: tenants, 32; self-employed workers in commerce, transportation, and other services, 13; wage laborers, 56; workers in cottage industries, eight; and total of them all, 109. It is worth noting that 52 per cent of the gainfully employed population are wage laborers.

6. The cultivated land in the village is owned by 25 landowners, 22 of whom have parasitical characteristics. Ten of them live in the Municipality of Baliuag, and the others live in such distant places as Manila. The largest landlord owns 20 hectares, but a majority of the landlords own one to four hectares. This pattern of landownership is known as *Lupang Tagalog*. Some landlords also own large holdings outside the village. Eighteen landowners purchased their land after World War II and the transfer of landownership occurs frequently.

7. Generally the tenants live near the farmland they cultivate. Their capital investment in land is nil, and their investment in equipment is quite small. Thirty-four of the 36 farming households keep *kalabaw*, and the average number of *kalabaw* per household is 1.3.

8. The village is served by the Angat River Irrigation System, the largest national irrigation project in the Philippines. Ninety-three per cent of the total farm area of the village is irrigated, but due to the slight relief of the land surface only 59 per cent of the land is utilized for double-cropping.

9. Although irrigation water is systematically controlled by the ARIS up to the level of the sub-laterals, maintenance of branch canals and distribution of irrigation water at the village level are not managed effectively. Much damage is caused by water shortage as well as by water-logging.

10. The paddy fields were formerly single-crop land but the spread of the early-maturing and non-seasonal varieties of rice since 1960 has made double-cropping possible in this area.

11. The traditional transplanting method, *ordinario*, is common in the village. The more effective *masagana* method was tried and showed promise of becoming popular, but in 1964 its use declined because it required more expense and labor than the *ordinario*, imposing a burden on tenants.

12. Farm productivity is low, although this area belongs to the leading agricultural region in the country. The standard yield per hectare is 50 to 55 cavans for regular crops and 35 to 40 cavans for secondary crops. In years of crop failures the yield is far below the standard.

13. In the processes of production there is a distinct division of labor. Plowing, harrowing, leveling, making seedbeds, fertilizing, and weeding are performed by cultivators, while bundling seedlings, transplanting, reaping, piling bundles of palay into *mandala*, and threshing are performed entirely by hired labor.

14. In most cases only heads of households are the domestically supplied labor. Female members of the farming households work as hired farm workers, but not on the farms of the households they belong to.

15. Farming households in the neighborhood exchange labor for plowing, harrowing, and leveling work.

16. The hired labor force consists mainly of heads of farming and non-farming households and their family members in and outside the village, and partly of migrant workers who come from other municipalities and provinces seasonally. These wage workers form labor gangs under

the leadership of foremen called *kabisilya,* and are engaged in transplanting, preparing seedlings, reaping, and threshing on a contract basis. The wages are decided on the basis of the size of paddy fields and they are paid in cash for transplanting and in kind for reaping and threshing. In the case of secondary crops, the wages paid for reaping and threshing are a proportion to the amount of harvested crops.

17. Six of the 36 farming households are tenants of two landlords. Thirty-seven per cent of the tenants have been cultivating the same land since before World War. II.

18. The farm rent varies according to oral contracts and is influenced by the terms concerning the sharing of farming expenses and the interest rate on debts owed to landlords. If expenses for irrigation water, seeds, transplanting, fertilizers, and harvesting are shared equally by landlord and tenant, the rent is usually 45 or 50 per cent.

19. The most common type of rent is the sharing of crops, but two tenants pay rents fixed in cash or in kind. The payment of fixed rents is expected to increase in the future.

20. When they live far away, landlords entrust the management of their land to farm overseers or to intermediaries who pay fixed rents to them.

21. Rarely do landlords intervene in tenants' management of farms.

22. When the replacement of a tenant takes place, it is not uncommon for the new tenant to pay his predecessor a sum of money which may be regarded as a kind of premium for renting land.

23. Disputes between landlords and tenants are not infrequent, but in most cases the tenants are the losers.

24. Although they are not strictly enforced, a series of tenancy and land reform acts have contributed toward reducing farm rents to some extent. Under the present circumstances, however, the transition from share rent to fixed rent is unlikely to be beneficial to tenants.

25. Under the present tenancy system, on land with the standard yield the tenant's share is generally 13 cavans of palay per hectare for the regular crop and 10 cavans for the secondary crop. Often the tenant's share is not sufficient to meet the domestic needs of his household. Furthermore, many tenant households cannot retain any rice at all after paying rent and interest because of their heavy indebtedness.

26. Credit for peasants is provided partly by the Rural Bank, but mainly by landlords. Interest rates differ considerably, but not infrequently tenants are charged up to 100 per cent per annum.

27. Peasants often sell their share of the crop to fill immediate needs for money, even though the rice sold is not surplus but part of the stock required for domestic consumption. Since it is thus difficult for peasants to retain rice for their own consumption, a majority of them purchase rice later when the market price is unfavorable.

28. Most of the farming households are heavily dependent on off-farm work for their livelihood, and in substance they are proletarianized.

29. The actual time when the labor force is employed is short. For instance, the number of days when heads of farming households are engaged in agriculture does not exceed 200 a year. From February to June, the bulk of the labor force in the village is completely idle.

30. Economic stratification in the village is horizontally structured, and there are no distinct difference among strata. This fact is reflected in political relations in the village.

31. Families in the village are related with one another by cognatic kinship system and by *compadrazgo*. Apparently there is no hierarchical relationship among kins.

32. The low level of the economy in the village, compared with nearby villages, is reflected in the way that the barrio fiesta is celebrated.

33. The landlord-tenant relations are impersonal, and landlords do not intervene in social relations in the village.

34. The communal features of the village society have been almost lost. Yet individual farming households as units of management have not established the initiative in controlling the processes of production. The village society puts pressure on farming households in such matters as the division of labor and the distribution of some portion of the crops to non-cultivating members of the village society. Such pressure serves to protect the lives of villagers against deprivation by landlords.

PART III
Land and Peasants in Central Luzon: Generalized Conclusions

CHAPTER XIV

Factors Hindering Agricultural Productivity

This region is one of the principal agricultural zones in the Philippines benefitting from a large-scale national irrigation project, as well as favorable topography and climate, and a short distance to the marketing center. It is surprising, therefore, to find the levels of agricultural technology and productivity in this region not much higher than the national average. In spite of the extensive network of irrigation canals, large tracts of land remain dependent on rain because, with only one exception, no efforts have been made to eliminate a slight relief of the land surface. Although the ARIS is the largest irrigation project in the country, irrigation water is not sufficient and the area is often hit by drought. On the other hand, paddy fields remain flooded during the rainy season, resulting in reduced crops. Although agricultural extension workers and demonstration farms are located nearby, little improvement has been seen in the methods of selecting seeds, fertilizing, and transplanting. Furthermore, damage due to insects, rats, and other pests is considerable. As for agricultural implements, mechanical power has been introduced into some processes, such as plowing and threshing, but the *araro, suyod,* and *lilik* remain the basic farm tools. Thus, farm productivity in Barrio Kabukiran remains 35 to 45 cavans of palay per hectare. What are factors causing such low productivity, and why are there few signs of development in this region which is the most important rice-growing zone in the Philippines?

First, we shall examine factors attributable to the landed class. Most landlords who own land in this village are small- and medium-size ones living outside the village. Only one of the small landlords living in the Municipality of Baliuag was seen making direct efforts to increase farm productivity, and thereby farm rents, through such means as improving land with hired bulldozers and visiting farmland often to supervise the operation of his tenants. Other landlords whether living in the municipality or in Manila did not have a positive interest in managing their farmland. Most of the landlords are mainly engaged in commerce and other businesses, have parasitical characteristics, and make no efforts to invest additional capital in the land or to improve farm operations although they do seek higher farm rents. When they employ *namumuisan* or *katiwala,* landlords rarely visit their land in the village. Even the landlords who are heavily dependent on farm rents were heard to say, "I know growing *dayatan* means a higher income, but I cannot do it because my land is elevated and it is difficult to obtain water. Leveling land is expensive," or "I recommend the *masagana* method to my tenants, but they decline to accept it because they find weeding troublesome."

Such attitudes of the landlords do not seem to have been affected by the fact that the transition from sharehold to leasehold began in July 1964 in the neighboring Municipality of Plaridel in accordance with the land reform legislation of President Macapagal. The landlords are optimistic about the chances of the law not being executed thoroughly.

Second, we shall examine factors attributable to cultivators. Farming households which cultivate small areas of farmland and pay high farm rents are far from being able to think of expanding farm production through increased investment in agricultural implements and improved methods of farm operation. Between 1958 and 1960, for example, there were some indications that peasants in this village would adopt the *masagana* system, but in 1964 it has disappeared from the scene. Reasons for the unpopularity of the *masagana* system are many. First, wages for transplanting are 40 to 50 per cent higher than in the *ordinario* method and half of the wages is shared by tenants. Second, considerable labor is required for irrigation water control, weeding, and fertilizing. Third, since most of the increased crops are taken by landlords for rent and interest payments, the increased farming expenses on the part of peasants do not result in the corresponding increase in incomes.

Introduction of the *dayatan* is hoped for as a means to increase employment opportunities, but no efforts are being made to create the conditions, such as improved irrigation and leveled land, which are necessary for *dayatan* growing.

A most impressive fact for this writer was that peasants did not have any will at all to increase the level of productivity of the land they cultivate. It is too much to expect peasants to have a positive desire for increased productivity, yet it is puzzling to see them doing nothing when it is quite obvious that a little more care and effort could prevent reduced crops. There are many such cases, but a few examples will suffice.

(1) Plants remained flooded for one week right after transplanting because the cultivator made no outlet in the dike when ordinary rain, not a typhoon, continued to fall for one or two days. The cultivator in this case did not live in the village but commuted from outside. When he came to see the paddy field one week after the rain the damage to the crop was already obvious.

(2) There were many cases in which reaped palay, spread out for drying, were covered by water because cultivators in adjacent paddy fields allowed water to overflow from their fields. As a result, the threshing yield was reduced and the quality of the rice deteriorated. Peasants themselves were heard saying, "If I had inspected the paddy field more often and filled in openings in the dike, I could have avoided such damage."

(3) It is customary to make *sipok* and pile them into *mandala* after reaping. In this process large amounts of palay are scattered, for the traditional varieties have a tendency to shatter. Simply spreading out canvases or mats on the ground would have collected such shattered palay, but only a few peasants take the trouble of doing so.

(4) Most peasants use part of their harvest as seed. Even if they cannot afford to buy government-certified seed, they can easily select better seed by the salt water method, but they do not do so. Taking poor care of seedbeds results in a shortage of seedlings, and this writer often saw peasants buying seedlings from other peasants at the time of transplanting.

Needless to say, it is the land system that fosters such an attitude in the peasants. Tenancy acts have been repeatedly legislated but high farm rents in kind have remained almost unchanged. The heavy pressure of landlords, pointed out many times since the Bell Report, still bears on peasants. This pressure by landlords does not come from high rent alone. Since most peasants are in heavy debt to them, the landlords can demand large portions of the crop shares belonging to the peasants. As was mentioned in Chapter VII, it is not rare that even at harvest time peasants have little palay left after paying debt to landlords. The provision in the Agricultural Tenancy Act guaranteeing a minimum 15 per cent share of crops for peasants is a dead letter in reality.

It is unreasonable to expect peasants to have a spontaneous willingness to increase productivity of land for under present circumstances the increased output from improved productivity is taken away by landlords. Since landlords do not meddle with peasants' incomes from work other than tenant farming, peasants make efforts to increase their incomes by concentrating their own and their families' labor on self-employed small businesses and wage work rather than increase farm productivity through such means as intensifying labor in their land and better fertilizing. Thus, peasants' input of labor in their land stands at the minimum level, sometimes below that level.

A fact we should pay special attention to is that for peasants to increase their net shares of crops is not necessarily to increase ostensible returns.

In Chapter XII, this writer mentioned that large portions of crops are taken away by non-cultivating villagers in accordance with the custom of *pulot* and *pumpong,* and that cultivators are often not present at the scene of harvesting. For peasants to obtain several gantas of rice from other villagers' land rather than an ostensible increase in their shares of crops, which will never be theirs, is sure to enrich their livelihood. This point will be elaborated on in Chapter XVI.

Anyway increased productivity of land does not bring much benefit to peasants who are suffering from high rents and heavy indebtedness. Contrarily, not to increase ostensible productivity does contribute toward improving the livelihood of peasants. Under such circumstances peasants cannot be expected to take a forward looking attitude and to be promoters of increasing productivity. Herein lies the greatest factor hindering agricultural productivity. We may say that this factor works not only in the landlord-tenant relations directly but also in the communal features of the village community.

According to information obtained recently it is said that a remarkable change in agricultural productivity has been occurring in this area. That is, in September 1966 the Pilot Rice Production and Extension Project was started in the Municipality of Baliuag through the joint effort of the Philippines and the Republic of China. Eighteen members of the Chinese Rice Technical Mission were stationed in the Municipality of Baliuag and established demonstration farms in each of 19 barrios, including Kabukiran. Intensified extension services were carried on particularly regarding adoption of new varieties, IR-8 and BPI-76, and of improved practices such as straight-row planting, adequate application of fertilizer, proper water management and so on. It is reported that in 1967 several farms in Kabukiran, which followed the improved practices, realized yields of 125-140 cavans of IR-8 per hectare. (*The Development of a Pilot Rice Production Demonstration Center in Baliuag, Bulacan* [n.p., n.d.]) It is certain that this governmental extension work has been done in an effective manner, but the actual response of the tenants and landlords remains unknown. Since we have seen that the *Masagana* system had once been tried and then abandoned under the present agrarian relationships, this writer is not yet inclined to be fully optimistic concerning this change.

It will be shown in the future whether this change is rooted firmly or not, of course the result will depend, at least in part, on the effectiveness of implementing agrarian reforms.

CHAPTER XV

Evolution of the Land System

1. Changes in the Landed Class

Generally speaking, studies in the economic history of the Philippines lag behind those in other fields of Philippine history. Especially, studies in the historic development of the landlordism which characterizes the land system in the Philippines today have not been sufficient.

It has been agreed that the development of landlordism in the Philippines paralleled the extension of commercial agriculture in the nineteenth century, but how today's stratum of big landlords came into existence is not known clearly yet. So far as Central Luzon is concerned, we may assume several types of development of the big landlords: First, land grants under the Spanish colonial rule;[1] second, land accumulation by merchants, especially Chinese Mestizos, in the course of development of the commercial economy in the nineteenth century;[2] and third, land consolidation by commercial capital in the 1920's and 1930's.[3] Yet regional differences in the development of big landlords and the historical connection between the types offered above have remained to be fully explored. To clarify these points, it is necessary to trace the historical character of individual landlords, but such case studies have not been undertaken so far. In the present survey this writer could not gather extensive data on the historic characteristics of landlordism, but he would like to offer a few generalizations.

There are three types of landholding in this region. The first is church and friar-owned estates which came into existence through land grants by Spanish kings in the seventeenth century and which were later enlarged through donations by peasants. The Buenavista Estate[4] is typical

---

[1]Allen, 54-55; and Pelzer, p. 90.

[2]Edgar Wickberg, "The Chinese Mestizo in Philippine History," *Journal of Southeast Asian History*, V-1 (1964), 75-76.

[3]Albert Kolb, "Die Reislandschaft auf den Philippinen," *Petermanns Geographische Mitteilungen*, LXXXVI-4 (1940), 118.

[4]This estate was granted to San Juan de Dios Hospital in Manila by Queen Isabella in 1682. It was 27,408 hectares in area and stretched over the three municipalities. See Chap. IV, n.1.

of such estates in this region. Under the American rule friar land was purchased by the government and redistributed to peasants, but church land has not yet been affected. It is difficult to know the exact area of land owned by the Roman Catholic Church, but it is undoubtedly the biggest landlord in this region, as we have seen the case of the Municipality of Baliuag.[5]

The second type of landholding is owned by parasitical landlords who came into existence not later than the nineteenth century and who are influenced by the moral attitudes of commercial capitalism. The size of these estates is sometimes several hundred hectares, and such land is managed by *katiwala* or *namumuisan*. This strata of landlords has tended to disintegrate rapidly in the past half century, especially since World War II. There are several factors contributing to this disintegration. First, the division of legacies into equal portions among siblings is the rule among the Catholics. Although this rule is not always observed very strictly and, as was mentioned earlier, joint ownership by family members called *comunidado* works to prevent disintegration, yet among families in the upper stratum the division of legacy into equal portions is quite common and is the biggest factor in the disintegration of large landholding. Second, since the stock market is underdeveloped in the Philippines, small and medium landlords have difficulty in finding profitable and stable businesses in which to invest their capital. Thus surplus capital accumulated in the villages is unlikely to be invested in the industrial sector. However, landlords in the upper stratum are enticed to invest their capital through various factors such kinship. They often sell land to get cash for investment in non-agricultural sectors such as commerce, industry, and real estate. Third, the requirements for expenditure on education must be considered. Even in the villages, families in the upper stratum want their children to be engaged in such socially prestigious occupations as lawyers, doctors, and engineers. Educational careers at leading universities in the United States or Europe are regarded as a prerequisite for climbing up the social ladder in such occupations. Hence, the higher the social stratum, the greater the expenditure on education. Landlords in the upper stratum often sell their land piecemeal to secure funds for their children's education abroad. Fourth, the history of agrarian

---

[5]Pelzer estimated that the church-owned land totalled at least 70,000 hectares as of 1938. Pelzer, pp. 90-91.

unrest, especially the collapse of the landlord-dominated hierarchy during the Hukbalahap-HMB disturbance, is vivid in the memories of old large landlords. Such landlords have fears and anxiety more or less over the future of ownership of tenant farms.

The third type of landholding is owned by the middle class, such as merchants or government officials who bought land from landlords of the second type with their savings. The holding ranges from several hectares to 30 or 40 hectares. Most of the landlords in Barrio Kabukiran belong in this category. Some are absentee landlords, but most supervise tenants in farm management without employing *katiwala*. A few of the landlords depend heavily on farm rents for their incomes and try to increase farm rents by strengthening their control over tenants.[6] But a majority of them derive their livelihood from non-agricultural sectors and have little desire to increase their incomes from farmland through such methods as the expansion of farmland, increased productivity of land, and stronger supervision of tenants. What, then, do the purchase and holding of farmland mean to these landlords? The price of farmland per hectare is now 6,000 to 7,000 pesos, but the landlord's share of the crop is about 25 cavans per hectare for a normal crop year and about 10 cavans for a poor crop year, so that his annual income from one hectare of land is 150 to 350 pesos, sometimes below the interest return on money deposited at the bank.[7] It is true that the landlord often can charge high interest on money loaned to tenants as well as receive farm rents, but it is usually difficult for him to collect all the principal and interest from tenants. Holding farmland as an investment, therefore, is not necessarily profitable for the landlord. It may be said that this strata wants to own land as a means of obtaining social status[8] and economic security, with only secondary importance attached to possible profits from an increase in land price.

Recent trends show that while the first type of landholding is relatively stable, the second type of landholding has been increasingly breaking down into the third type of small landholding. Thus, today we can hardly observe the trend toward land concentration which was reported by Allen

[6]Such was once considered the typical behavior pattern of small and medium landlords. (TAKAHASHI, "Recent changes," 69.)

[7]The interest rate of commercial banks is five to nine per cent, averaging 6.3 per cent.

[8]In Philippine society, whether in cities or in villages, ownership of farmland is an extremely important factor in social status.

for Central Luzon in the 1930's.[9]

2.   Changes in the Tenancy

The general pattern in the *kasama* relations in the Philippines is that landlords pay land taxes and half of farming expenses, advance money to tenants for the payment of farming expenses, and collect both farm rents and advanced money at harvest time. As was mentioned earlier, landlords in this region rarely show positive interest in the management of farmland through inspection of farmland, or supervision and guidance of tenants. Only a few landlords attempt to increase farm productivity in a positive manner such as long-term capital investment in land improvement, and a majority of the landlords have strong parasitical characteristics.

On the other hand, tenants usually own houses, some farm implements, and *kalabaw,* but are dependent on loans from landlords for living expenses until harvest time as well as for their shares of farming expenses. Since tenants often have no crops left after paying their debts to landlords, it is natural that they should not make any efforts to increase productivity of the land they cultivate, although they are willingly interested in earning from side work, as was noted in the preceding chapter. Landlords sometimes discharge tenants when the latter's care of rice plants is extremely inferior to that in the surrounding paddy fields. But so long as tenants attend to their crops in a normal way, they are not responsible for crop failures however bad they may be; such failures are blamed on nature, not on the tenants. What tenants do under such circumstances is to input minimal labor into the land so as not to be discharged by their landlords, but with the attitude that the amount of crops is no serious concern of theirs. So long as they remain tenants, they can expect to borrow living expenses from their landlords; in other words, the minimum level of livelihood of tenants is ensured by landlords.

Tenants, in fact, share very little responsibility or risk for farm management, and they are more like agricultural wage workers, although they are called share tenants. For tenants, the significance of farmland is not so much as the means to create profits from agricultural production, but as the basis of the landlords' guarantee for their livelihood. Under the present circumstances where the peasants are almost helpless against the overwhelming power of the landlords, and where the principal sources of agricultural credit for peasants are landlords and moneylenders, the intro-

[9]Allen, 55-56.

duction of leaseholds will result in higher farm rents decided arbitrarily by landlords, higher interest rates, and increased responsibility for farm management on the part of tenants. When a landlord tried to impose leasehold on his tenants, as described in Chapter VII, it was very natural that the tenants were strongly opposed to it. It is for the same reason that peasants do not always favor introduction of leasehold in accordance with the Land Reform Code.

We have discussed the social relations between landlords and tenants in detail in Chapter XII. Generally speaking, contacts between landlords and tenants are limited to economic matters. It cannot be said that the relations are the hierarchical ones of domination-subordination or master-vassals like the landlord-tenant relations in China under the old regime or in India. In this region where absentee landlords are predominant, family-type benevolent elements do not play an important role in the landlord-tenant relations.

It is worth noting that the landlord-tenant relations in the Philippines are moderate compared with those in other Asian countries or in prewar Japan. For example, landlords accept the custom in which villagers other than their tenants carry home the part of the crops gleaned at the sites of reaping and threshing, though this means a decrease in return for the landlords. Besides, when they collect debts of tenants only out of the crops from the land they rent, and not from the tenants' incomes from wage work. Allen reported on tenants working at the households of their landlords, forced contributions and additional service on landlords' birthdays, various kinds of fines, forced attendance to church, and restrictions on visitors.[10] Worcester reported on landlords using family members of tenants as something like domestic slaves when debts were not repaid.[11] Such practices are no longer observed today, at least not in this region.

This is one aspect of the characteristics of the landlord-tenant relations in the Central Luzon Plain. The pressure of surplus population supporting landlordism has been rapidly increasing, and *puesto,* the embryonic form of a premium for the privilege of renting land, has already appeared in Central Luzon (Chap. VII, Sec. 3). The increase in resumption of land by landlords is partly due to the existence of vast reserves of tenants. Under such circumstances, the deprivation of tenants by landlords could be more severe than it is. We do not have data sufficient to explain this

[10] Allen, 62-63.
[11] Dean Worcester, *Slavery and Peonage in the Philippine Islands* (Manila, 1913).

phenomenon, but a few reasons may be offered. For one thing, landlords in Central Luzon generally have strong parasitical characteristics and their dependence on farm rents is low. For another, the consciousness and energy of peasants seem to be effective in preventing landlords being arbitrary. The landlords, who have learned a lesson from the past agrarian unrest, seem to have prepared a safety valve against the outbursts of discontent.

CHAPTER XVI

Formation of the Surplus Labor Force

This writer has pointed out that a large amount of the wage labor force in Philippine villages is employed by small farms rather than by large estates.[1] In general, however, the demand for wage labor cannot be expected to be large in an agricultural economy based on family farms. The question of how such a large force of wage workers can stagnate in the villages remains to be answered.

First, the actual demand for wage labor in the villages is far larger than would be expected. In this region an extensive labor market exists because many villagers work in Manila for a long term as skilled and unskilled workers, and many others work in other provinces as migratory agricultural and non-agricultural workers. However, what is more important is local employment. In Barrio Kabukiran many villagers are self-employed in businesses such as *karitela* driving and small stores, and in cottage industries such as *buntal* hat-weaving, but the largest proportion of villagers are engaged in agricultural work, especially agricultural wage labor rather than self-employed agricultural work.

Let us examine the nature of the demand for wage labor by small farms. Even small farms are highly dependent on wage labor for the main farm work. It must be emphasized that employed labor is introduced not to meet a shortage of family labor on small farms, but because family labor is hardly expected to play any significant role in production, even on small farms. This attitude is socially given, so that individual cultivators cannot decide what processes of production shall be performed by wage labor. Thus, wage labor remains an important factor in farm production. This is a noteworthy characteristic of the production structure in the rice-growing region of Central Luzon.

We must remember that another important factor in the large demand for wage labor is the double-cropping in this region. Double-cropping not only doubles employment opportunities, but also lengthens considerably the time when wage labor is in demand. The intermingling of single- and double-crop lands and the difference of one to one and a half months

[1]TAKAHASHI, "Peasantry Disintegration," 40.

in the crop calendar between the south and north sides of the ARIS district further prolong the work season. Double-cropping serves also to level seasonal fluctuations of employment. For example, in the case of agricultural laborers who both transplant and harvest palay, if they work in double- and single-crop land on both the south and the north sides of the Angat River, there exists demand for their labor more or less all year round except for two and a half months from early April to late May and from early through middle December (see Fig. 4).   Of course, employment usually is obtained through introductions by relatives and friends, so it is impossible for anyone to be employed throughout the season (Chap. IX, Sec. 3). Nevertheless, it must be noted that double-cropping lengthens the time in which agricultural laborers are employed.

Second, demand for wage labor in the villages is created and expanded by the production structure under the present land system. Peasants and their family members are underemployed, and yet they depend on wage labor for farm operation. Hitherto, this was explained on the assumption that peasants cannot meet the demand for labor in the peak time because of their extensive farming methods, lack of planning in labor allocation, and low labor productivity.[2] This explanation, however, is not convincing in view of the fact that peasants absent themselves from the land they cultivate at the very time when they hire wage workers. It is not enough to seek to find the explanation of the anomaly in the individual peasants' way of operating their farms. Rather, we must appreciate the fact that the anomaly has been created and expanded by the present tenancy system.

In principle, paying more wages to hired labor means an increase in farming expenses and, therefore, a decrease in returns. But in the landlord-tenant relations in Central Luzon, as was mentioned in Chapter XIV, landlords ruthlessly collect debts out of tenants' shares of crops, but usually do not touch peasants' and family members' incomes from side work. What is most important for peasants, then, is not their incomes from farms under their operation, but their incomes from wage work and businesses other than tenant farms. Hence, the ostensible amount of crops subject to sharing with landlords is of little importance to tenants. Such being the circumstances, the payment of wages to hired labor is not simply an addition to farming expenses. What is most important, such

[2]TAKAHASHI, "Chinrōdō no keisei" (Formation of the Wage Labor Force) in M. SUMIYA, ed., *Firippin no rōdō jijō* (Labor Conditions in the Philippines) (Tokyo, 1961), p. 234.

payments increase the amount of wages left in the village. Here is the economic basis for the distinct division between family labor and wage labor and for peasants tending to depend on wage labor for farm work. It is for this reason that peasants and their families work on each other's farms rather than making efforts to improve the operation of their own farms. Furthermore, it is quite reasonable from the viewpoint of peasants that communal forms of labor exchange such as *suyuan* or *palusong* are generally seen only in plowing and harrowing, expenses for which are to be shared entirely by peasants. It is clearly to their advantage that peasants seek to minimize expenses which are borne by themselves alone, and to maximize the wage expenses which are divided between landlords and tenants.

As mentioned above, it has often been observed that labor exchange among farming households is the common pattern in Philippine agriculture (see Chap. XII, n. 4). Such an arrangement may be applicable to a society where owner farmers are dominant, but not to agriculture production under the tenancy and social relations which exist in Barrio Kabukiran. In this village hired labor plays a leading role in farm production, not merely a role supplementary to family labor. Thus, we can say the logic of family farms are no longer valid in this region.

As was explained above, the present heavy dependence on hired labor has been brought about by the *kasama* system. If the *kasama* is replaced by the fixed rent system, tenants will make efforts to reduce farming expenses and their dependence on family labor will be increased. Thus, it is possible to anticipate that progress in implementation of the Land Reform Code followed by the increase in leaseholders will enhance the self-sufficiency of farm labor in villages of this region.

When the pattern of wage labor described above came into existence, and to what extent it is widespread in the Philippines, remain to be clarified, but at least in the rice-growing region of the Central Luzon Plain it is observed extensively.

Third, the present condition of peasants is a result of a historical development, which is in parallel with the development of landlordism as was described in the preceding chapter. In view of (1) the statistical analyses of the four censuses in 1903, 1918, 1939, and 1948,[3] (2) Rivera and McMillan's report that 15 per cent of agricultural laborers, 27 per cent of tenant farmers, and 83 per cent of part-owner farmers said their

---

[3]TAKAHASHI, "Wage Labor", pp. 208-220.

fathers were owner farmers,[4] and (3) the development of palay production, sugar estates and modern sugar centrals,[5] this writer has concluded that the rapid disintegration of landholding by peasantry occurred in the 1920's, although a considerable number of rural proletariats had already existed in Central Luzon at the beginning of this century.[6]

In the persent survey this writer could not obtain detailed data on the situation 50 years ago. But, as was mentioned in Chapter X, he did not come across either farming or non-farming families which had been owner farmers one or two generations before. In other words, it is clear that peasantry ownership was not the basic pattern of land tenure, and that a large number of workers without landholdings existed at the beginning of this century. On the other hand, as we have seen in the preceding chapter, large-scale landholding in this region came into existence during or before the nineteenth century.

In any case, it is difficult to trace adequately the process of disintegration of the peasantry in this region. But it is safe to say that the proletarianization of peasants began at a very early date under Spanish colonial rule. It has been mainly demanded for wage labor by peasants that has absorbed rural wage labor. On the other hand, feudalistic landholding families have not transformed themselves into agricultural capitalists but have become parasitical landlords. Under such circumstances employment in agriculture has not been sufficient, the expansion of farms based on leasehold has been impossible, and the peasantry themselves have moved toward proletarianization. Furthermore, since the development of industrial capital was retarded, the wage labor force has stagnated in the villages and has not migrated to the cities. Thus, villages have become reservoirs of surplus population, and the peasantry has become increasingly tied to the land instead of being discharged from agriculture. Being chronically underemployed and forced to take side jobs, peasants are in substance proletarianized.

[4]Rivera and McMillan, *Central Luzon,* p. 64.
[5]For example, see Allen, 55-56.
[6]TAKAHASHI, "Wage Labor", p. 215.

CHAPTER XVII

Characteristics of Village Structure

Kasama peasants and agricultural laborers are basic elements in village structure, under the extensive system of parasitical landownership. Peasants are highly dependent on wage works for their incomes and are, in substance, proletarianized. The economic differences among peasants are not marked, nor are the differences of social status, and there is frequent alternation between peasants and wage laborers. So we may say there is no distinct difference between peasants and wage laborers, even though the latter are employed by the former. Thus, the socio-economic stratification is decidedly horizontal, and the status hierarchy does not appear in the village.

On the other hand, we can observe several strata in the landed class: large landlords who tend to invest their capital in industry, and medium-size and small ones who have strong parasitical characters. *Katiwala* and *namumuisan* intervene between landlords and tenants as bulwarks of the former. Landlords exercise control over tenants not only through renting the land, but also through supplying credit, operating rice mills, and renting farm tractors and *telyadora*. Therefore, the most fundamental antagonism exists between landlords on the one hand and peasants and rural laborers on the other. This antagonism locally emerges as opposition between the village and the town rather than as conflict within the village.

Although the village is favored by irrigation and other basic agricultural facilities, both landlords and peasants lack the positive attitude toward farm management under the present tenurial relations, so that their input of capital and labor in land is small, and impetus for the expansion of farm production are almost lost. A large surplus population sustained by demand for wage labor by peasants stagnates in the village. Both peasants and agricultural laborers are in chronic underemployment.

These characteristics are not limited to the village surveyed, but are widely observed in the Central Luzon Plain where land is generally owned by absentee landlords.

Meanwhile, in the basic pattern for rural families in the Philippines, the household is large in size, family unity is strong and tinged with patriarchal characteristics, and family members give economic assistance to one another. This writer has also appreciated such strong family ties as one of the principal factors leading to latent surplus population in Philippine villages.[1]

On closer observation of rural families, however, one discovers that family relations are not uniform, but different among different strata. The principle of inheritance which divides a legacy into equal portions is observed rather strictly by the upper stratum like *propiyetaryo*. On the other hand, the middle strata families such as small landlords disintegrate rapidly in regard to the size of household, but, as was described earlier, the division of a legacy does not take place immediately after the death of a proprietor. Rather, the legacy is owned jointly by kins, who help one another without asserting the title to their portions of the inheritance. The actual division may be delayed for many years. In the case of peasants, who account for a large majority of the rural population, the family disintegrates easily into nuclear families because family property poses no complicated problems and because inexpensive and simple houses can be built freely on parts of tenant land.

The interdependence of nuclear families, one on another, is observed in kinship groups, as well as in communal groups based on local propinquity. What is more, this interdependence seems to work more effectively in communal groups than in kinship. The *compadrazgo* relations based on the Catholic rituals also broaden familial associations in village society, but it should not be overevaluated. This custom seems to be primarily a reinforcing element in communal association.

Thus, in association of village society kinship and the landlord-tenant relations are important factors, but communal relations based on local propinquity are a greater determining factor. It is often observed that new migrants who have no relatives in the village are not discriminated against, but are accepted by village society without difficulty. What distinguishes one village from another appears to be the geographical unity of the village, further strengthened by the fact that villagers belong to the same religious group with a common village chapel and a common patron saint.

Although the stratified composition of village society is horizontal, the pressure of village society on individual farming household is found in various aspects of life, including the landlord-tenant relations. As we have seen in Chapter XII, villagers are allowed to be engaged in *pulot*,

[1]TAKAHASHI, "Peasantry Disintegration," 44.

pumpong and other customs. Of course, the history of struggles fought in Central Luzon by *Kapatiran,* KPMP, PKM, Hukbalahap, and HMB cannot be ignored as an important factor in the preservation of these customs. The peasants' organization, once a powerful social group in the 1950's, and yet their influence is still strongly felt today.[2]

Furthermore, as was repeatedly mentioned, the division of labor in the process of farming, *pulot* and *pumpong* are socially established customs which landowners and cultivators cannot eliminate. It is rational enough for the villagers to give one another opportunities for employment and incomes through these customs, because they are designed to increase retained incomes. We must remember, however, that these are not cultivators' own choice.

From the foregoing we can conclude that farming households have not established their initiative as economic units yet, and that the regulation of individual farming households by the village society is quite strong. It is difficult to generalize about the source of such regulation, but we can observe that one of the important factors is the idea of *hiya* (shame)[3] as a sense of propriety in human relations in village society. This *hiya,* as social pressure and tension, regulates the behavior of individual villagers. When villagers act against the social norm, they are immediately branded *walang hiya* (shameless). Being called *walang hiya* seriously damages one's respectability. The basis for the existence of such regulation is that it serves to protect the livelihood of the peasants from pressure of the landlords. In this regard it may be safe to say that communal relations in the village are still an essential factor in the processes of agricultural production.

It is worth emphasizing that peasants' demand for wage labor leading

---

[2]It is often reported in the newspapers and magazines that the "Huks" have revived and its activities are still rampant in the provinces of Central Luzon; e.g., "The Huk Situation," *Philippine Free Press,* August 6, 1966, 2-3, 41-44, 69, "The Present Huk Situation in Central Luzon," *Manila Daily Bulletin,* June 2-6, 1967, "Huks," *Life* (Asian Edition), July 10, 1967, 20-25. Even a former leader of the movement termed the situation a resurgence of the Hukbalahap; see William J. Pomeroy, *Guerrilla and Counter-Guerrilla Warfare* (New York, 1964), pp. 71-72. This writer is not willing to associate all anti-governmental activities or social unrest directly to the Hukbalahap-HMB movement. However it is undoubtedly true that the soil for such resistance is nourished by the present socio-economic conditions of peasantry.

[3]F. Lynch, "Social Acceptance" in his *Four Readings on Philippine Values,* pp. 16-17; Hollnsteiner, "Reciprocity," p. 31; and J. Bulatao, "Hiya," *Philippine Studies,* XII (1964), 424-438. The Japanese equivalent to *hiya* is *sekentei* (sense of one's face or sense of reputation), which we can easily observe in the rural society of Japan.

to the stagnation of a surplus population in the village has been created and expanded by the present structure of agriculture, and that the demand is reinforced by the social structure of village, especially by the regulations of communal relations. In the structural characteristics of wage labor in the village one can find the interconnection between production relations and social relations and a clue to comprehensive understanding of factors in both stagnation and development of social structure.

The representativeness of the Philippine villages in general by the rice-growing village in Central Luzon sketched in this monograph remains to be confirmed by further surveys and accumulation of monographs. At this stage, however, it may be said that the village surveyed suggests one direction of development for village structure in the Philippines, in view of the following conditions: Central Luzon is primarily characterized by large absentee landlords; the old system of landholding has disintegrated and small and medium landlords have been newly born; being close to Manila, the village is strongly affected by the development of monetary economy; the village having been once the scene of agrarian unrest, peasants' class consciousness is keen and the old hierarchical order centering around landlords is challenged; the level of education is high; and agricultural productivity is more or less higher in comparison with other regions.

APPENDICES

BASIC DATA ON HOUSEHOLDS

No.	Name of head	Remarks	Area of holding	Gross area planted to palay	No. of Kalabaw	Size of household	Age and occupations of members of household							
							1	2	3	4	5	6	7	8~
1	Serrano, Sixto	Barber, *Sarisari*	1.0	2.0	1	7	34HAL	(31)SB	(11)-	(9)-	(6)-	4-	(2)-	
2	Corpus, Antonio		5.0	8.0	3	7	39A	(38)-	(18)P	(15)-	(12)-	5	(2)-	
3	Dizon, Andres	Pedicab	1.0	1.0	-	1	35TAL							
4	Cortes, Pedro		2.5	2.5	(1)	4	80A	(73)-	16LA	7-				
5	Balao, Jesusa	Non-farming	-	-	-	3	(54)LB	(33)LB	2-					
6	Villanueva, Pablo	*Kabisilya*	2.5	5.0	1	5	60ALC	(56)-	22LA	12-	(10)-			
7	Villanueva, Domingo		2.0	4.0	-	5	25ALC	(22)B	(5)-	(3)-	1-			
8	Corpus, Mario	Non-farming	-	-	-	3	24L	(20)L	(2)-					
9	Corpus, Josefina	Non-farming	-	-	-	2	(67)-	(64)B						
10	Corpus, Lope	Non-farming	-	-	-	2	80-	(32)B						
11	Corpus, Gabriel		1.5	3.0	1	8	42AL	(41)L	19L	(18)B	15L	12-	(10)-	8-
12	Corpus, Carlos	Non-farming	-	-	-	3	25L	(27)L	(53)L					
13	Tolentino, Tomas		1.0	2.0	1	3	24AL	(31)L	(1)-					
14	Tolentino, Roberto		2.0	4.0	1	6	26AL	(28)L	7-	(5)-	3-	(1)-		
15	Dizon, Manuel	Office clerk	4.5	4.5	1	5	44OA	(34)-	(10)-	7-	(4)-			
16	Araneta, Paulino	*Karitela*	2.5	5.0	2	3	46KA	(44)-	19K					

17	Castillo, Ricardo		2.2	3.2	1	4	23AL	(21) B	20W	(1) –	(7) –	(4) –	1–	5–
18	Mendez, Angel	Tractor driver	5.0	5.0	1	7	43AL	(36) –	10–	8–				
19	Araneta, Ramon		–	–	–	4	24DL	(30) L	(11) –	8–				
20	Sanchez, Arcadio		1.5	3.0	1	5	26AL	(26) –	7–	(5) –	3–			
21	Serrano, Sabino		1.5	1.5	1	4	28AL	(19) –	3–	(1) –				
22	Serrano, Pastor		1.9	1.9	1	2	29AL	(23) L							
23	Marcos, Pastor	*Karitela*	2.5	5.0	1	8	43KA	(38) –	17KL	14–	12–	10–	8–	5–
24	Hilado, Agustin		4.0	6.0	1	11	40AC	(37) L	65A	(63) –	[(17) S]	14–	11–	(9) –, 5 –; (3) –, (1) –
25	Castillo, Paterno		1.3	2.5	1	7	42ALC	(40) L	31L	6–	4–	2–	1–	
26	Alonzo, Jesus	*Karitela*	1.3	2.0	1	8	38KAL	(43) –	20AL	(18) L	(16) L	(9) –	(7) –	(4) –
27	Isidro, Miguel	Pedicab	1.3	2.5	1	2	23TAC	(25) L							
28	Gonzales, Eugenio		3.5	7.0	2	4	30AL	(34) –	(3) –	1–				
29	Sanchez, Rodolfo	*Karitela*	5.3	9.1	2	9	47KA	(49) –	26L	(25) –	[(20) G]	18AL	16–	14LA, (9) –
30	Adeva, Lucas	Farming land outside village (*Kabisilya*)	1.5	3.0	–	3	43AL	(20) L	(1) –					
31	Gonzales, Mauro		3.0	5.0	2	7	43AL	(42) L	20AL	18L	16L	(9) –	6–	
32	Dalisay, Lorenzo	*Karitela*	5.0	10.0	1	6	22KAL	(43) –	(20) L	18LA	16LA	10–		
33	Tolentino, Conrado	Non-farming	–	–	–	5	60L	(50) L	24L	17L	(16) L			
34	Moreno, Felipe	Cantina	3.5	5.5	1	5	59A	(40) S	[25R]	[22R]	[17R]			
35	Soriano, Arthur		2.5	2.5	1	6	52AL	(50) –	17AL	14–	13–	11–		

No.	Name of head	Remarks	Area of holding	Gross area planted to palay	No. of Karabaw	Size of household	Age and occupations of members of household							
							1	2	3	4	5	6	7	8~
36	Sison, Lucas		2.5	2.5	1	6	34AL	(43)L	(12)-	8-	(7)-	(3)-		
37	Bonoan, Jaime	Pedicab	5.0	6.8	3	7	43AC	(38)-	23ML	20TLA	18LA	(14)G	10-	
38	Abello, Nestor		2.5	4.0	(1)	4	33AL	(28)L	6-	4-				
39	Manahan, Raul	Barrio Captain	1.5	1.5	1	8	36AL	(36)L	16-	(14)-	12-	10-	8-	6-
40	Manahan, Emilio	Non-farming	-	-	-	5	44L	(38)B	20-	18L	(8)-			
41	Hilado, Mario		1.5	3.0	1	5	25AL	(29)-	4-	(3)-	1-			
42	Hilado, Daniel		1.3	2.5	1	11	60AL	(58)B	(30)B	20LA	(20)L	(13)L	(11)-	(10)-, (8)- (7)-, 3-
43	Hilado, Edmundo		2.5	5.0	1	6	38AL	(32)-	12-	8-	7-	2-		
44	Hilado, Leon		2.0	4.0	1	2	27AL	(49)-						

Remarks: 1.   Parentheses around the number of *kalabaw* indicates borrowed ones.
2.   Abbreviations for occupations: A=Cultivator,   B=*Buntal* hat weaver,   C=Carpenter,   D=Tractor driver, G=Store-clerk,   H=Barber,   K=*Karitera* driver,   L=Farm laborer,   M=Sawmill worker,   O=Office clerk, P=Beautician's apprentice,   R=Auto repairman,   S=*Sarisari* and *cantina* keeper,   T=Pedicab driver,   W= Wireman.
3.   Age in parentheses indicates female.
4.   Age and occupation in brackets indicate a member of family working away from home.

GLOSSARY

(Sp. .... Spanish: *Italics* .... Tagalog)

Ahente	Agent, dealer. (Sp. ágente)
Aling	Hypocoristic term of direct address to aunt or elder female.
Arrendador	Intermediary renter of large-scale estate. (Sp. arrendar=to rent or to lease)
ARIS	Angat River Irrigation System.
Bakuran	Homelot, backyard. (*bakod*=fence)
Banâ	Lowland, pool, puddle, marsh.
Baníg	Mat of *buri* palm.
Batalis	Exchange of labor between farming households.
Bayan	Town, nation; Town-proper.
Bayanihan	Work for a time for somebody.
Binato	An early maturing variety of palay for *dayatan*.
Bisita	Barrio chapel.
Bunot	Pull, root out; Pulling and bundling of seedlings.
Buwís	Tax, tribute, fixed rent.
Búwisan	Rented or leased land; Fixed rent tenancy.
Cavan	Grain measure equal to 75 liters. One cavan of palay is 44 kilograms.
Comunidado	Joint ownership of property.
Dayatan	Secondary crop of palay.
Dayudayuhan	Cultivation of land outside village where one lives. (*dayo*=go to another place)
Ganta	Grain measure equal to one twenty-fifth of a cavan.
Gapas	Harvest, reaping.
Giík	Thresh cereals especially by trampling upon them.
Hampás	Blow, strike, thresh.
HMB	*Hukbong Mapagpalaya ng Bayan*=National Army of Liberation.
Huk	*Hukbalahap* and/or HMB.
Hukbalahap	*Hukbong Bayan Laban sa Hapon*=National Anti-Japanese Army.
Intan	A non-seasonal variety of palay.
Isinasalang	Light plowing. (*salang*=light touch)
Kabisilya	Head or foreman of a team of wage laborers. (Sp. cabeza=head)
Kaingin	Hilly land grubbed and cleared of trees and bush for cultivation.
Kalabáw	Water buffalo.
Kalesa	Calash: Two-wheeled carriage usually for two to three persons.
Kalsada	Street, avenue: Town-proper.
Kanál	Canal, ditch.
Kapatiran	A peasants' union organized in the late 1920's in Bulacan and Pampanga.
Karitela	Two-wheeled carriage usually for six to nine persons.

Kasamá	Partner in business: Tenant or landlord in share tenancy.
Kátiwalá	Overseer especially of a landed estate. (*tiwala*=trust)
KPMP	*Katipunan Pambansa ng Magbubukid sa Pilipinas*=National Union of Peasants in the Philippines.
Kubo	Farm hut.
Lala	To weave, e.g., a hat or mat.
Lateral	Branch of irrigation canal, sub-main canal.
Lilik	Serrated sickle for reaping palay.
Magsasaka	Farmer, peasant.
Manananim	Transplanter.
Mandalá	Cylindrical stack of palay stalks ready for threshing.
Mang	Hypocoristic term of direct address to uncle or elder male.
Manggagapas	Reaper.
Manggagawa	Laborer, cultivator.
Masagana	A method of linear transplanting of palay. (*masagana*=prosperous)
Mitra	Church land. (Sp. mitra=bishop's miter, bishopric)
Namumuisan	Tenant in *buwisan* tenancy: Intermediary landlord renting land from landowner in *buwisan*.
Namumulot	Those who do *pulot*.
Namumumpong	Those who do *pumpóng*.
Namumunot	Those who do *bunot*.
Ninang	Godmother.
Ninong	Godfather.
Ordinario	Traditional method to transplant palay seedlings.
Pahingá	Rest, repose, intermission.
Palagad	Dry season crop.
Palay	The rice plant: Unhulled rice.
Palusong	Cooperative work based on exchange of labor between farming households.
Panag-araw	Regular crop of palay, summer crop.
Pilapil	Dike or levee in paddy field.
PKM	*Pambansang Kaisahan ng mga Magbubukid*=National Peasants' Union.
Poblacion	Downtown district of a municipality.
Propiyetaryo	Landlord, landed family. (Sp. propietario=man of property)
Puesto	A sort of right of cultivation of rented land or premium to acquire the privilege. (Sp. puesto=place, position, post)
Pulot	Pick up, gleaning.
Pumpóng	Harvesting worker's bringing home a sheaf of reaped palay.
Punong-sugò	Headman of a team of farm laborers. (*punò*=leader, head: *sugò*=delegate)
Saka	Farm cultivation, tillage.
Salahan	Embranchment of irrigation ditches. (*salà*=filter, dam)
Sangá	Branch, irrigation ditch.
Sapà	Creek, brook, small stream.
Sarisari	Small general store. (*sarisari*=miscellaneous, various)

Silong	Space below the house floor.
Sipok	Stack of reaped palay.
Suyod	Harrow, comb.
Suyuan	Ingratiation, working into another's favor.
Telyadora	Large-size threshing machine. (Sp. trillador=thresher)
Utang	Debt, indebtedness.
Utang na loob	Debt inside oneself, sense of gratitude.
Uwáy	A specy of rattan, material for *buntal* hat.
Wagwag	A late maturing variety of palay.

REFERENCES

Abueva, Jose V. *Focus on the Barrio*. Manila: Institute of Public Administration, Univ. of the Philippines, 1960.

Allen, James S. "Agrarian Tendencies in the Philippines." *Pacific Affairs*, XI (1938), 52-65.

Anderson, James N. "Some Aspects of Land and Society in a Pangasinan Community." *Philippine Sociological Review*, X (1962), 41-58.

"Ang Bagong Halaga ng Bayad sa Patubig ay di Nakabibigad sa mga Magsasaka." Santa Cruz River Irrigation System Office. n.d.

Aragones, Santos G. "Tenancy, Land Use and Farm Management Practices in Macalong, Asingan, Pangasinan." *Philippine Agriculturist*, XL (1956), 147-162.

Arce, Wilfredo F. "Social Organization of the Muslim Peoples of Sulu." *Philippine Studies*, XI (1963), 242-266.

Arens, Richard. "Animism in the Rice Ritual of Leyte and Samar." *Philippine Sociological Review*, IV-1 (1956), 2-6.

Balak na Tuwirang Pagbibili ng Asienda Buenavista. n.p., 1941.

Balinguit, Teodoro B. "Palay Marketing on the Farm Level in Nueva Ecija, 1955-1956." *Philippine Agriculturist*, XLII (1958), 18-35.

Bategui, B. and J. Sumagui. "The Food Supply Situation in the Philippines, CY 1965-66." *Statistical Reporter*, XI-4 (1967), 11-22.

Blair, E. H. and J. A. Robertson. *The Philippine Islands 1493-1898*. Cleveland: A. H. Clark Co., 1903-1909.

Bulatao, Jaime C. "Hiya." *Philippine Studies*, XII (1964), 424-438.

Caintic, C. U., J. C. Santa Iglesia and H. von Oppenfeld. *Management Practices, Costs and Returns of Sugar Cane Farms in the Victorias Milling District*. College, Laguna: College of Agriculture, Univ. of the Philippines, 1962.

Case, George S. "The Geographical Regions of the Philippine Islands." *Journal of Geography*, XXVI-2 (1927), 41-52.

Cater, Sonya D. *The Philippine Federation of Free Farmers: A Case Study in Mass Agrarian Organization*. Ithaca: Cornell Univ., 1959.

Coller, Richard W. *Barrio Gacao, a Study of Village Ecology and the Schistosomiasis Problems*. Quezon City: Community Development Research Council, Univ. of the Philippines, 1960.

Conklin, Harold C. *Hanunóo Agriculture, a Report on an Agriculture System of Shifting Cultivation in the Philippines*. Rome: Food and Agriculture Organization, 1957.

Corpuz, Onofre. *The Bureaucracy in the Philippines*. Manila: Institute of Public Administration, Univ. of the Philippines, 1957.

———————————. *The Philippines*. Englewood Cliffs, N.J.: Prentice-Hall, 1965.

Covar, Prospero. *The Masagana/Malgate System of Planting Rice: A Study of an Agricultural Innovation*. Quezon City: Community Development Research Council, Univ. of the Philippines, 1960.

Crippen, Harlan R. "Philippine Agrarian Unrest: Historical Background." *Science and Society*, X (1946), 337-360.

Cutshall, Alden. "Problems of Landownership in the Philippines." *Economic Geography*, XXVIII (1952), 31-36.

———————————. "Regionalism in Philippine Agriculture." *Journal of Geography*, LXI-7 (1962), 289-296.

Darrah, L. B. *Marketing of Farm Products in the Philippines*. College, Laguna: College of Agriculture, Univ. of the Philippines, 1958.

The Development of a Pilot Rice Production Demonstration Center in Baliuag, Bulacan. n.p., n.d.

Diaz, Ralph C., Horst von Oppenfeld and Judith von Oppenfeld. *Case Studies of*

Farm Families, Laguna Province, Philippines. College, Laguna: College of Agriculture. Univ. of the Philippines, 1960.

Diaz-Trechuelo. Maria L. "The Economic Development of the Philippines in the Second Half of the Eighteenth Century." *Philippine Studies,* XI (1963), 195-231.

——————. "Eighteenth Century Philippine Economy: Agriculture." *Philippine Studies,* XIV (1966), 65-126.

Eggan, Fred. "Some Aspects of Cultural Changes in the Northern Philippines." *American Anthropologist,* XLIII (1941), 11-18.

——————. "The Sagada Igorots of Northern Luzon," in *Social Structure in Southeast Asia,* ed. George P. Murdock. Chicago: Quadrangle Books, 1960, pp. 24-50.

Encarnacion. Vicente. "Leadership in a Benguet Village." *Philippine Studies,* IX (1961), 571-583.

Fox, Robert B. "Social Class," in *Area Handbook on the Philippines,* Vol. I. Chicago: Univ. of Chicago for the Human Relations Area Files, Inc., 1956, pp. 437-467.

Golay, Frank. *The Philippines: Public Policy and National Economic Development.* Ithaca: Cornell Univ. Press, 1961.

Gorospe, Vitaliano R. "Christian Renewal of Filipino Values." *Philippine Studies,* XIV (1966), 191-227.

Hart, Donn V. "Barrio Caticugan: A Visayan Filipino Community." Dissertation, Syracuse Univ., 1954.

——————. *Philippine Plaza Complex; a Focal Point in Cultural Change.* New Haven: Yale Univ., 1955.

Hartendorp, A. V. H. "The Proposed Land Reform Act." *Journal of the American Chamber of Commerce of the Philippines,* XXXIX (1963), 164-185.

Hayden, Joseph R. *The Philippines: A Study in National Development.* New York: MacMillan, 1955.

Hollnsteiner, Mary R. *The Dynamics of Power in a Philippine Municipality.* Quezon City: Community Development Research Council, Univ. of the Philippines, 1963.

——————. "Reciprocity in the Lowland Philippines," in *Four Readings on Philippine Value,* compiled by Frank Lynch. Quezon City: Ateneo de Manila Univ. Press, 1964, pp. 22-49.

Houston. Charles O., Jr, "Rice in the Philippine Economy 1934-1950." *Journal of East Asiatic Studies,* III (1953), 13-76.

——————. "Customs Associated with Rice Cultivation in the Philippines." *Journal of East Asiatic Studies,* III (1954), 287-296.

Huke, Robert. "Maloco: A Representative Aklan Barrio." *Philippine Sociological Review,* IV-2, 3 (1956), 23-28.

——————. ed. *Shadows on the Land: An Economic Geography of the Philippines.* Manila: Bookmark, 1963.

Hunt, Chester L. *et al. Sociology in the Philippine Setting.* Manila: Alemar, 1954.

Ienaga, Yasumitsu. "Rice Culture and Irrigation Systems in the Philippines," in *Water Resource Utilization in Southeast Asia.* Kyoto Univ. Publications, Symposium Series, III. Kyoto, 1966, 177-183.

Jacoby, Erich H. *Agrarian Unrest in Southeast Asia.* Bombay: Asia Publ. House, 1961.

Jagor, Feodor. *Travels in the Philippines.* London: Chapman & Hall, 1875.

Jose, F. Sionil. "The Philippine Agrarian Problem." *Comment,* No. 9 (1959), 85-143.

Kaut, Charles. "The Principle of Contingency in Tagalog Society." *Asian Studies,* III (1965), 1-15.

Kolb, Albert. "Die Reislandschaft auf den Philippinen." *Petermanns Geographische Mitteilungen,* LXXXVI (1940), 113-124.

Kroeber, Alfred L. "Kinship in the Philippines." *Anthropological Papers of the American Museum of Natural History,* XIX-3 (1919), 73-84.

Kroef, Justus M. van der. "Patterns of Cultural Conflict in Philippine Life." *Pacific Affairs,* XXXIX (1967), 326-338.

——————. "Philippine Communism and the Chinese." *China Quarterly,* No. 30 (1967), 115-148.

Kurihara, Kenneth K. *Labor in the Philippine Economy.* Stanford: Stanford Univ. Press, 1945.

Ladejinsky, Wolf. "Agrarian Reform in Asia." *Foreign Affairs,* XLII (1964), 445-460.

Le Roy, James A. *Philippine Life in Town and Country.* New York: Putnam's Sons, 1905.

Levinson, G. I. *The Workers' Movement in the Philippines.* Scholarly Book Translation Series, No. 662. Annapolis, Maryland: Research and Microfilm Publications, Inc., n.d. (Original: Moscow, 1957.)

Lynch, Frank, S. J. "Continuities in Philippine Social Class." *Historical Bulletin,* VI (1962), 40-51.

——————. "Social Acceptance," in *Four Readings on Philippine Value,* compiled by him. Quezon City: Ateneo de Manila Univ. Press, 1964, pp. 1-21.

——————. "Trend Report of Studies in Social Stratification and Social Mobility in the Philippines." *East Asian Cultural Studies,* IV (1965), 163-191.

"Management and Operation of Irrigation and Drainage Systems in the Philippines." Paper presented at the Irrigation Symposium of the Bureau of Public Works, Manila, August 1963.

McHale, Thomas R. "The Philippines in Transition." *Historical Bulletin,* VII (1963), 293-300.

Miller, Hugo H. *Principles of Economics Applied to the Philippines.* Boston: Ginn & Co., 1932.

Nurge, Ethel. "Land Ownership, Occupation and Income in a Leyte Barrio." *Philippine Sociological Review,* IV-2, 3 (1956), 15-22.

——————. *Life in a Leyte Village.* Seattle: Washington Univ. Press, 1965.

Nydegger, W. F. and C. Nydegger. *Tarong: An Ilocos Barrio in the Philippines.* New York: John Wiley, 1966.

Oppenfeld, Horst von, Judith von Oppenfeld, J. C. Santa Iglesia and P. R. Sandoval. *Farm Management, Land Use and Tenancy in the Philippines.* College, Laguna: College of Agriculture, Univ. of the Philippines, 1957.

Pal, Agaton P. "A Philippine Barrio: A Study of Social Organization in Relation to Planned Cultural Change." *Journal of East Asiatic Studies,* V (1956), 333-486.

——————. *The Resources, Levels of Living and Aspirations of Rural Households in Negros Oriental.* Quezon City: Community Development Research Council, Univ. of the Philippines, 1963.

——————. "Aspects of Lowland Philippine Social Structure: Social Structure and the Economic System." *Philippine Sociological Review,* XIV (1966), 31-39.

"The Peasant War in the Philippines." *Philippine Social Sciences and Humanities Review,* XXIII (1958), 373-436.

Pelzer, Karl. *Pioneer Settlement in Asiatic Tropics.* New York: American Geographical Society, 1945.

Piron, Jorge. "Land Tenure and Level of Living in Central Luzon." *Philippine Studies,* IV (1956), 391-410.

Pomeroy, William J. *Guerrilla and Counter-Guerrilla Warfare.* New York: International Publishers, 1964.

Quintana, Emilio U. "An Economic Analysis of Philippine Rice Farms." *Economic Research Journal,* XII (1965), 134-147.

Quintana, Vicente U. "Palay Marketing Practices of Farmers in Gapan and San

Antonio, Nueva Ecija, 1955-1956." *Philippine Agriculturist,* XLI (1957), 327-343.

Republic of the Philippines, Dept. of Labor. *Employment of Migrant Labor (Sacadas) in the Sugar Industry in Negros Occidental.* Manila, 1956.

Republic of the Philippines, Office of the Economic Coordination. *Report and Recommendations of the Advisory Committee on Large Estates Problems.* Manila, 1951.

——————————. *Report of the Special Committee on Land Settlement and Title Issuance and Clearance.* Manila, 1951.

Rivera, Generoso and Robert McMillan. *The Rural Philippines.* Manila: Philippine Council for U.S. Aid, 1952.

——————————. *An Economic and Social Survey of Rural Households in Central Luzon.* Manila: Philippine Council for U.S. Aid, 1954.

Romani, John H. "The Philippine Barrio." *Far Eastern Quarterly,* XV (1956), 229-237.

Roosevelt, Theodore. "Land Problems in Puerto Rico and the Philippine Islands." *Geographical Review,* XXIV (1934), 182-204.

Ruttan, Vernon W. "Tenure and Productivity of Philippine Rice Producing Farms." *Philippine Economic Journal,* V (1966), 42-63.

——————————, A. Soothipan and E. C. Venegas. "Changes in Rice Production, Area, and Yield in the Philippines and Thailand." *Economic Research Journal,* XII (1965), 181-201.

Sacay, Orlando J. "The Philippine Land Reform Program." *Philippine Economic Journal,* II (1963), 169-183.

Scaff, Alvin H. *The Philippines Answer to Communism.* Stanford: Stanford Univ. Press, 1955.

Schul, Norman W. "A Philippine Sugar Cane Plantation: Land Tenure and Sugar Cane Production." *Economic Geography,* XLIII (1967), 157-169.

Scott, William H. "Growing Rice in Sagada." *Philippine Economic Journal,* II (1963), 85-96.

Sibley, Willis E. "Leadership in a Philippine Barrio," in *Social Foundations of Community Development,* eds. S. C. Espiritu and C. Hunt. Manila: R. M. Garcia, 1964, pp. 308-315.

——————————. "Persistence, Variety and Change in Visayan Social Organization: A Brief Research Report." *Philippine Sociological Review,* XIII (1965), 139-144.

——————————. "Economy, Social Organization and Directed Change: The Philippines." Paper read at the Symposium on Modernization in Rural Areas, the Eleventh Pacific Science Congress, Tokyo, August 1966.

Soroñgon, A. *A Special Study of Landed Estates in the Philippines.* Manila, 1955.

Spencer, J. E. *Land and People in the Philippines: Geographic Problems in Rural Economy.* Berkeley: Univ. of California Press, 1952.

Sturtevant, David R. "Sakdalism and Philippine Radicalism." *Journal of Asian Studies,* XXI (1962), 199-213.

Takahashi, Akira. "Modernization of the Peasant Community in Central Luzon, Philippines." Paper read at the Symposium on Modernization of Rural Areas, the Eleventh Pacific Science Congress, Tokyo, August 1966.

Takigawa, Tsutomu. "Landownership and Land Reform Problems of the Philippines." *Developing Economies,* II (1963), 58-77.

Taruc, Luis. *Born of the People.* Bombay: People's Publ. House, 1953.

Tiglao, Teodora V. *Health Practices in a Rural Community.* Quezon City: Community Development Research Council, Univ. of the Philippines, 1964.

Tiongson, Fabian A. *Improved Merchandising of Selected Farm Products.* Quezon City: Community Development Research Council, Univ. of the Philippines, 1964.

University of the Philippines, College of Agriculture. *Rice Production in the Philippines.* College, Laguna: College of Agriculture, Univ. of the Philippines, n.d.

U.S., Dept. of State. *Report to the President of the United States by the Economic Survey Mission to the Philippines.* Washington, D.C., 1950.

U.S., Mutual Security Agency, Special Technical and Economic Mission. *Philippine Land Tenure Reform: Analysis and Recommendations.* Manila, 1952.

Vega, Gloria R. "The Expenditures of Incomes of 100 Families in Canlalay, Biñan, Laguna, 1955." *Philippine Agriculturist,* XLI (1957), 344-356.

Villanueva, Buenaventura M. *A Study of the Competence of Barrio Citizens to Conduct Barrio Government.* Quezon City: Community Development Research Council, Univ. of the Philippines, 1959.

Wernstedt, F. L. and J. E. Spencer. *The Philippine Island World: A Physical, Cultural and Regional Geography.* Berkeley: Univ. of California Press, 1967.

Wickberg, Edgar. "The Chinese Mestizo in Philippine History." *Journal of Southeast Asian History,* V (1964), 62-100.

——————. *The Chinese in the Philippine Life, 1850-1898.* New Haven: Yale Univ. Press, 1965.

Worcester, Dean C. *Slavery and Peonage in the Philippine Islands.* Manila: Bureau of Printing, 1913.

Wurtel, David. "The Philippine Rice Share Tenancy Act." *Pacific Affairs,* XXVII (1954), 41-50.

——————. "Philippine Agrarian Reform under Magsaysay." *Far Eastern Survey,* XXVII (1958), 7-15, 23-30.

PUBLICATIONS IN JAPANESE

BABA Keinosuke, ed. *Firippin no kinyū to shihon keisei* (Finance and Capital Formation in the Philippines). Tokyo: Institute of Asian Economic Affairs, 1961.

HAMA Hidehiko. "*Firippin nōgyōmondai eno kisokōsatsu* (A Basic Approach to Philippine Agricultural Problems)," in *Chirigaku ronbunshū* (Geographical Studies). Tokyo: Kokon Shoin, 1961, pp. 538-556.

IENAGA Yasumitsu. "Firippin no kokuei kangaisoshiki ni okeru suirihi mondai (The Irrigation Cost Problems in the National Irrigation System in the Philippines)." *Ajia keizai,* VIII-11 (Nov., 1967), 64-75.

——————. "Firippin no inasaku keiei to suiri chitsujo (Irrigation in Rice Producing Areas in the Philippines)." *Nōgyō keizai kenkyū,* XXXIX (1967), 132-139.

KAWADA Tadashi. "Teikaihatsushokoku no keizaikōzō to kindaika no kadai (Economic Structure of the Underdeveloped Country and the Problems of Modernization: The Philippine Case)." *Keizaigaku kenkyū,* XXXII-2 (1966), 11-26.

TAKAHASHI Akira. "Firippin nōgyō no dōkō (Recent Changes of the Philippine Agriculture)." *Tōyō bunka,* No. 30 (1961), 49-104.

——————. "Firippin no tochikaikaku (Land Reform in the Philippines)," in *Ajia no tochikaikaku* (Land Reforms in Asia), ed. OWADA Keiki. Tokyo: Institute of Asian Economic Affairs, 1962, pp. 277-362.

——————. "Chinrōdō no keisei (Formation of Wage Labor Force)," in *Firippin no rōdō jijō* (Labor Conditions in the Philippines), ed. SUMIYA Mikio. Tokyo: Institute of Asian Economic Affairs, 1962, pp. 159-286.

——————. "Firippin nōson shakai no jakkan no mondai (Problems Relating to the Peasantry Disintegration in the Philippine Rural Society)." *Kaigai jijō,* XI-8 (1963), 38-45.

——————. *Chūbu Luzon no beisaku nōson* (A Rice-Growing Village in Central Luzon). Tokyo: Institute of Asian Economic Affairs, 1965.

——————. "Firippin nōson kōzō ni kansuru ichi kōsatsu (A Note on the Socio-Economic Structure of the Philippine Villages)." *Tōyō bunka,* No. 43

(1967), 49-76.

TAKIGAWA Tsutomu. "Firippin tochiseidoshi josetsu (An Introduction to the Historical Study of Land Tenure of the Philippines with Special Reference to the Philippine Revolution)." *Nōgyō sōgō kenkyū,* XVII-1 (1963), 1-64.

—————————. "Firippin no sonraku shakai kōzō (Social Structure of the Philippine Villages)," in *Kaigai shokoku ni okeru nōgyō kōzō no tenkai* (Agricultural Stucture in a Changing World—Typical Cases of Foreign Countries), eds. MATOBA Tokuzō and YAMAMOTO Hideo. Tokyo: National Research Institute of Agriculture, 1966, pp. 3-49.

—————————. "Firippin no tochikaikaku ni kansuru oboegaki (A Note on Land Reform in the Philippines)." *Ajia keizai,* V-10 (1964), 2-16.

—————————, ed. *Firippin no tōgyō* (Sugar Industry in the Philippines). Tokyo: Institute of Asian Economic Affairs, 1966.

UENO Fukuo. Nōson jittai chōsa hōkoku (Survey Report on Desa Tjimahi, Soekaboemi, Bogor). Batavia: Office of Military Administration, 1944.

UMEHARA Hiromitsu. "Manila kinkō ni okeru sosaisaku no jittai (Vegetable Farming in the Suburban Districts of Manila)." *Ajia keizai,* VIII-1 (1967), 33-46.

—————————. "Firippin no beisaku nōson (A Rice-Growing Village in the Philippines: Survey Report on Barrio Tubuan, Pila, Laguna)," in *Ajia no tochiseido to nōson shakai kōzō II* (Land Systems and Village Structures in Asia II), eds. TAKIGAWA Tsutomu and SAITO Hitoshi. Tokyo: Institute of Asian Economic Affairs, 1967, pp. 141-205.

INDEX

Abello, Nestor, 66, 79

Acuña, P., 72

Adeva, Lucas, 53

Agrarian unrest, 9, 135, 139, 146n; *see also* Huk

Agricultural Credit Administration, 87

Agricultural Credit and Cooperative Financing Administration, 87n

Agricultural extension worker, 59, 60n, 129

Agricultural Land Reform Code of 1963, 38, 75-77, 87n, 138, 142

Agricultural laborer, 29, 30, 61-65, 97-100, 103-104, 144; *see also* Hired labor *and* Farm labor

Agricultural Productivity Commission, 59, 60n, 75, 82

Agricultural Tenancy Act of 1954, 26, 70, 75n, 76, 77, 81, 131

Agriculture
in Baliuag, 13
in Central Luzon, 7-9, 24
commercial, 3, 133
crop calendar, 54-56, 103, 141; see also *Dayatan, Palagad* and *Panagaraw*
damages on crop, 47, 59, 120, 129, 131
farm equipment, 21, 52-53, 57, 129; see also *Telyadora* and Tractor
productivity, 43, 47, 59, 78, 129-133
patterns of cultivation, 54-60
vegetable-growing, 19, 102, 105, 119

Ahente, 34, 38, 41, 72

Allen, James S., on land concentration, 137n, 143n; on land grant, 32n, 134n; on landlord-tenant relations, 138; on *pomata* and *postura,* 79n

Alonzo, Jesus, 94

Anderson, James N., on Pangasinan village, 2n

Angat River, 13, 24, 49

Angat River Irrigation System (ARIS), 13, 15, 19, 24, 31, 32, 49-52, 56, 58, 103, 129, 141; *see also* Irrigation

Angeles, T., 71

Apalit, Municipality, 32, 39

Araneta, Paulino, 62, 85, 94, 98, 115n

Araneta, Ramon, 98

Araro, 52, 58, 129

Arayat, Mt., 9, 25

Arrendador, 32, 40, 73, 74-75, 119; see also *Namumuisan*

Bakuran, 19, 59

Balagtas, R., 72

Balao, Jesusa, 98

Balinguit, Teodoro B., 2n

Baiuag, Municipality, 9-13, 26
climate, 15-17
cultivated area, 19
landlords of, 32-33
transportation, 15, 93-94

Bana, 15, 19, 37, 59, 98, 107

Barber 29, 45, 96, 101

Barrio, 4, 9, 27, 112

Barrio captain, 88, 97, 115-116

Barrio Charter, 27n, 115

Barrio council, 88, 115-116

Barrio school, 5, 18, 23, 96

Batalis, 61, 96, 110, 112, 120; *see also* Labor exchange *and* Palusong

Bategui, B., on food, 83n

Bayanihan, 120

Bell Report, 78, 131

Binato, see Palay

Bisita, see Chapel

Blair, E. H., on communal land, 119n

Bonoan, Jaime, 95, 104, 114

Boundary system, 94-95

Buenavista Estate, 32n, 134

Bulatao, Jaime C., on *hiya,* 146n

Bunot, 58, 65

Buntal hat, 12, 30, 37, 43, 95, 96-97, 100, 140
merchant of, 37, 40, 96

Bustos, Municipality, 17, 32n, 49, 93

Buwis, 39, 40, 66, 68, 69-71, 73-78

Buwisan, see Buwis

Buying station, 92

Cadastral survey, 23, 31